Economics Unmasked

 **Philip Bartlett Smith** was a American-Dutch experimental physicist. He taught for eight years in Brazil as a McCarthy-era exile, and later joined the University of Groningen as a Professor of Physics, where he remained until his retirement in 1988. He was a member of the Board of Pugwash Netherlands until 2003. He had a tense relationship with his native US, which he labelled "The Holy American Empire" and whose power policy he abhorred. After his retirement he concentrated on the subjects of deep concern to him: disarmament, environment and energy, poverty and world economics. He was co-editor with S. E. Okoye, J. de Wilde and P. Deshingkar of *The World at the Crossroads: Towards a sustainable, equitable and livable world* and the editor of *Dimensions of Sustainability,* proceedings of the INES Congress 'Challenges of Sustainable Development', Amsterdam, August 1996. Philip passed away on December 15, 2005.

 **Manfred Max-Neef** is a Chilean-German economist in the field of international development. His key works are *From the Outside Looking in: Experiences in 'Barefoot Economics'* and *Human Scale Development,* the latter declared by the University of Cambridge as one of the 50 most important books on sustainability. He taught in Berkeley in the early 1960s and was visiting professor in several US, Latin American and European Universities. He also worked for several UN agencies, and between 1994 and 2002 was Vice-Chancellor of the Universidad Austral de Chile in Valdivia. In 1983 he received the Right Livelihood Award (Alternative Nobel Prize). He holds honorary doctorates from Jordan, Colombia, Argentina and the US, and has been the recipient of the University Award of Highest Honour from Japan. He is the Director of the Economics Institute of the Universidad Austral de Chile.

Economics Unmasked

From power and greed to
compassion and the common good

Philip B. Smith & Manfred Max-Neef

green books

First published in the UK in 2011 by

Green Books
Foxhole, Dartington,
Totnes, Devon TQ9 6EB

Design by Jayne Jones
Cover design by Rick Lawrence and Jayne Jones
Diagrams by Rick Lawrence

ISBN 978 1 900322 70 6

Printed on Corona Natural 100% recycled paper by
TJ International Ltd, Padstow, Cornwall, UK

Contents

Dedication

To those who believe that life, love and happiness
are more important than the economy.

To those who believe that a more humane economy is possible.

To those who are willing to stop living better than others,
in order to start living well with others.

Acknowledgements

Our gratitude to Henny and Gabriela for their love, loyalty
and permanent encouragement.

Our admiration to Alethea Doran, the most professional and
rigorous editor we have ever come across.

Preface

The story behind this book

This book is the result of a long dialogue between a physicist and an economist.

Philip Smith, who obtained his PhD in Physics at the University of Illinois, taught for seven years in Brazil – an exile from the McCarthy era – and later for 25 years at the University of Groningen in the Netherlands. After his retirement he informed friends and colleagues that he had read "three full metres of books on economics", and that he was prepared to discuss the discipline. What motivated him was his deep and lifelong commitment to social justice. As a physicist he was a leading member of Pugwash, an anti-nuclear-proliferation organization, whose scope was beyond the mere limiting of nuclear weapons. His main concern was about ethical choices in society, the economy and the environment. During his navigation through those three metres of books, he realized not only that neoclassical economics was a pseudo-science full of inconsistencies and failings, as a consequence of its effort to look as similar as possible to physics, but also that the primary purpose of the discipline, in its neoclassical version, was to serve the function of defending the status quo of wealth and power. It was a discipline clearly divorced from any possibility of social justice.

In turn, I (Manfred Max-Neef) became an economist at the University of Chile, and started my academic career at 27 years of age, as a Lecturer in Berkeley during the early sixties. After my California period I worked for the Organization of American States and later for the FAO (Food and Agriculture Organization) and ILO (International Labour Organization) of the United Nations, in the field, in rural and urban areas of extreme poverty. It was there that one day, in a village of the Andean Sierra, I was standing in the mud and in front of me, also in the mud, was standing a thin man, hungry and jobless, with five children, a wife and a grandmother. While we were looking at each other I was overwhelmed by a sudden consciousness that I lacked a language that could make sense in such a situation. My whole discourse as a conventional academic economist was absolutely inadequate for me to say anything significant. I was used to diagnosis and analysis, but I was not used to understanding. I knew all about poverty and had all the statistics, yet there I was, speechless, when looking poverty in the face. It became clear to me that I had to invent a new language. That was the origin of my 'principles of barefoot economics', and my rebirth as an absolute dissident of mainstream economics due to its inability to interpret poverty and, hence, social justice.

It was just a matter of Jungian synchronicity that the paths of the physicist and the economist had to converge. The encounter occurred in August 1996 in Amsterdam during the Congress of Challenges of Sustainable Development organized by the International Network of Engineers and Scientists for Global Responsibility. Philip and I were together in a workshop and developed an immediate empathy. Long and lively conversations followed in the two evenings we spent together walking along the Amsterdam channels and drinking some fine Chilean wines. Our friendship was consolidated. We exchanged frequent correspondence, and about five years later the idea arose that we might try to write a book together with the purpose of revealing how economics would look behind its mask of a supposedly hard, value-free, mathematical science.

I invited Philip to come to Valdivia in Chile, where I was Rector of the University. He stayed for three months of intense, entertaining and often funny conversations about economics, social justice, transcendence, spirituality, chaos theory and quantum physics. We floated happily in a marvellous transdisciplinarity that brought us closer and closer to understanding the frustrated relationship between economics and the real world. We decided that Philip would write a draft of the first part of the book, concerned with the critical analysis of the development of economics, and I would later write an additional part, with proposals for a new economics coherent with the challenges of the twenty-first century. We discussed his drafts by mail, and we were in full agreement about the final versions that are presented in this book.

When the time came for me to produce my part, I travelled to Groningen to visit Philip and show him my contribution. Once again we were in full agreement, but unfortunately he was seriously ill at that time, and a few weeks later his heart abruptly weakened and he passed away on 15 December 2005. As a result he never saw the final product, but I am sure that wherever he is he approves of it. When I said goodbye to him, he told me: "Manfred, make sure that the book is published; I want it to be my final testimony to the world." I am, therefore, extremely happy that his testimony will endure.

The book is the work of both of us. However, Philip was mainly responsible for Chapters 2 to 8; I was mainly responsible for Chapters 1 and 9 to 13. Although through the text we mostly use the word 'we', in Chapter 4 the 'we' has been replaced by 'I' because the chapter's contents express a profoundly personal reflection of Philip about honesty and values. Nonetheless, it is a reflection with which I fully agree.

This joint intellectual and spiritual adventure with Philip has been one of the most enriching experiences in my life. It was also fascinating to personally witness how easy it is for natural scientists to discover the many inconsistencies and mathematical absurdities of economics once they decide to familiarize themselves with the discipline. His case was similar to that of Frederick Soddy, a Nobel Laureate in Chemistry, who in the early 1920s wrote a couple of books through which it became evident that he understood economics better than most economists; for this he was of course ridiculed and excommunicated by the economics establishment, and his books were banned from the reading lists of students. Today Soddy's truth remains untarnished, and I am sure that so will the truth of Philip Smith.

Manfred Max-Neef, Valdivia, Chile, January 2011

Introduction: the case for a new economics

Our vision of a just world motivated us to produce this critical analysis of economic thought at the beginning of the twenty-first century. In a just world, human beings on the whole treat each other fairly so that all may live in dignity, without fear and with adequate means for satisfying the universal needs of humankind. No truly just society has ever existed, of course. But not all societies are equally unjust. There are great differences in the degree of justice in different countries and in different segments of society within countries. This makes for a complicated, multidimensional picture. At the core, though, there is a simple relationship between the structure of a society and its measure of justice.

Stated succinctly, it is the distribution of economic and financial power that determines how just a society is. The more concentrated this power, the less just a society. This simple relationship is particularly relevant to the underlying economic paradigm of neoliberal economics, which exalts the unregulated market. Since an unregulated (so-called 'free') market leads irrevocably to the concentration of economic power, i.e. to injustice, it is clear that to build a better society that is closer to the ideal, one must look critically at the market paradigm and ask oneself if it cannot be replaced by a more humane alternative. This is the main goal of this book, which we hope will be of use to those who share our vision of a just world – not that it will be easy to bring such a world into being. Although there are now, as there have always been, many who dedicate their lives to justice, the desire for a just world is anything but widespread among those who have the most to say about humankind's fate: that is, those who have economic and financial power.

Politics and economics cannot be separated, but the focus of this book is on the relationship between justice and the economic organization of society. The focus is there because it is the economic structure of today's global world that generates the greatest obstacle to moulding a more just world society. Political power is subservient to economic power, simply because economic and financial power give political power to those who have it, and, inversely, those without economic power are bereft of the means to wield political power. Of course, economics aside, unjust political systems cause great suffering, but the political regime of a land is visible and can, in principle, be fought against. Not so the economic system, the workings of which are largely invisible.

In what are loosely called the capitalist countries we see a degree of regulation of markets, although for the last three decades a convergence toward deregulation has been taking place, particularly in the monetary and financial sectors. As already remarked, an unregulated market is certain to create an unjust division of power – because the market transfers more wealth and power to those who already have much of both, while depriving those without either of the possibility of defending themselves against exploitation and its concomitant injustice. Colonization, the plundering of poorer countries (referred to as 'the periphery' in developmental discourse) by the capitalist powers, was indeed initially promoted by political and military means. But it was fundamentally an economic arrangement, in which the poorer countries delivered cheap labour, raw materials and agricultural products, while serving as a market for finished products. That is also the function of what is presently called globalization, and its handmaiden, the much-vaunted 'level playing field'. Here, practically no military might is needed, but only largely invisible economic power, to continue unabated this centuries-old process of plunder. This explains why globalization is so popular, domestically and internationally, among those individuals and nations with the most wealth and power.

The economic system under which we live does more than force the great majority of humankind to live their lives in indignity and poverty. It also threatens all forms of life – indeed life itself. The merciless onslaught on the life-sustaining capacity of ecosystems brought about by the ten- to hundred-fold increase in production and the consequent poisoning and depletion of reserves in recent decades is not a chance property of the system. It is inherent in the system itself. It is a direct consequence of the view of life, human and non-human, fostered by neoliberal economic thinking – which, as a corollary of its fundamental *raison d'être*, the enrichment of the few, can recognize value only in material things. The obsession with growth of production, characteristic of this thinking, is not a mistaken conception that mainstream economists can unlearn. It is inherent in their view of life. Therefore another, equally important, motive for writing this book is to try to promote a new view of life itself, by presenting a cogent critique of the dominant economic paradigm, to help transform our society into one in which all forms of life will be protected against the onslaught. Only such a society can be *sustainable*. A socio-economic system based on the growth paradigm can never be sustainable.

We reject the facile idea that the organization of society that we wish to promote contradicts the principles of economics. It depends whose economic principles we are talking about. The etymology of the word economics (*oikonomia*, meaning housekeeping) suggests that this is the discipline that one would expect to lay down the rules needed to provide the very protection for which we are arguing. But economics as the discipline is now construed (generally excluding ecological economics) has no mechanism to provide this protection. It is dedicated to increasing production without limit, and the paradigm on which it is based postulates, incredible as it may seem, that ecosystems are invulnerable to damage at the hand of humankind. A further basic postulate is that nature has the capacity to provide humankind forever with an unlimited supply of raw materials. *Oikonomia*, instead, suggests that you take care that the 'house' is well provided for, for tomorrow and the future. But the neoliberal economist seems hell-bent on exploiting the 'house' to the limit, and is not interested in the future of life on Earth, beyond the next quarterly figures.

We have spoken of justice and sustainability. It may be that the two are not, in the short term, synonymous. But we have great difficulty in imagining a world where, for an extended period of time, society operates sustainably but without justice. The powerful resistance that mainstream economists, and the theories they defend, present to those who wish to forge a more just world and/or a sustainable world is not 'value-free' but inherently opposed to both justice and sustainability. The paradigm of modern economics is not housekeeping but exploitation (*chrematistics*, in Aristotle's sense – more about this in Chapter 2). Greedy human behaviour, which throughout all of human history has been condemned by all religions and all philosophical thought, is today considered laudable in the world of the mainstream economist. But one cannot be in favour of both greed and justice at the same time, nor can one defend the future of life by exploiting today, without limit, the riches of the world.

As we said, there is economics and economics. The greater part of this book is devoted to showing that, as the discipline of economics has evolved out of the various possibilities, theoretical constructions have been selected that support injustice. The economic arrangement of society is to the liking of those who profit most from it. And it is no coincidence that they are exactly those who wield the power – the power to maintain intact the arrangement that suits them. History shows no examples of the powerful voluntarily relinquishing their power to the powerless. So, writing these words may not move the contented to bring about change in the economic arrangement of the world. But words do have power, and perhaps the power of these words will help move humankind toward a better future.

Chapter 1

From knowledge to understanding

Life is an unending sequence of bifurcations: the decision that I take implies all the decisions I did not take. Our life is inevitably a permanent choice of one possibility out of an infinity of ontological possibilities. The fact that I was at a given place, at a very precise moment in time, when a given situation occurred or a given person appeared, may have had a decisive effect on the rest of my life. A few minutes earlier or later, or a few metres away in any direction, might well have determined a different bifurcation and, hence, a completely different life. As the great Spanish philosopher José Ortega y Gasset pointed out: "I am myself and my circumstance."

What holds for individual lives holds for communities and whole societies as well. Our so-called Western (Judaeo-Christian) civilization is the result of its own bifurcations. We in the West are what we are, but we could also have been something we are not. Let us then recall some of our decisive bifurcations.

Early in the thirteenth century, in Italy, a young man named Giovanni di Bernardone, while still very young and very rich, decides to radically change his life. As a result of his transformation, we remember him today under a different name: St Francis of Assisi. Francis, when he refers to the world, speaks of brother Sun and sister Moon; of brother wolf, and of water, fire and trees; and people as brothers and sisters as well. The world he describes and feels is a world where love not only is possible but makes sense and has a universal meaning.

Sometime later, also in Italy, we hear the resounding voice of the brilliant and astute Machiavelli, warning us that: "It is much safer to be feared than to be loved." He also describes a world, but in addition he creates a world.

The world we have today is not that of Francis, it is the world of Machiavelli. Francis was the route not navigated. The navigation we chose was that of Machiavelli, and inspired by it we have constructed our social, political and economic conceptions.

In 1487, another very young man, just 23 years of age, Francesco Pico della Mirandola, prepares himself for the public defence of his 900 theses about the concord between the different religions and philosophies. He refuses to enclose himself within the narrowness of just one doctrine. Convinced that truths are multiple, and never just single and universal, he longs for a spiritual renovation that can reconcile humanity.

Some years later Francis Bacon, a fervent believer in absolute truth and in the possibilities of certainty, invites us to torture Nature so that through the delivery of her secrets we can extract the truth.

Again, two worlds. One represents the route we navigated; the other the route we did not. We did not follow the way suggested by Pico della Mirandola. We opted for accepting Bacon's invitation, and, thus, we continue applying his recipe with efficiency and enthusiasm. We continue torturing Nature in order to extract from her what we believe to be the truth.

In the year 1600, Giordano Bruno burns at the stake, the victim of his pantheism, since he believes that the Earth is life and has a soul. All things, for him, are manifestations of life. Everything is life.

Three decades later, Descartes whispers: "Through my window, what I see are hats and coats covering automatic machines."

We did not navigate the route of Giordano Bruno. We chose that of Descartes, and, in that manner, we have witnessed the triumph of mechanism and reductionism.

For Galileo and Newton, the language of Nature is mathematics. Nothing is important in science that cannot be measured. We and Nature, the observer and the observed, are separate entities. Science is the supreme manifestation of reason, and reason is the supreme attribute of the human being.

Goethe, whose scientific contributions have been (unjustly) overshadowed because of his colossal achievements in literature and the arts, felt upset with what he believed to be the limitations of Newtonian physics. For Goethe, "science is as much an inner path of spiritual development as it is a discipline aimed at accumulating knowledge of the physical world. It involves not only a rigorous training of our faculties of observation and thinking, but also of other human faculties which can attune us to the spiritual dimension that underlies and interpenetrates the physical: faculties such as feeling, imagination and intuition. Science, as Goethe conceived and practised it, has as its highest goal the arousal of the feeling of wonder through *contemplative looking* (*Anschauung*), in which the scientist would come to see God in nature and nature in God."[1]

Two worlds once more: another bifurcation. We are still under the spell of the overpowering lustre of Galileo and Newton, and have chosen not to navigate the route of a Goethean science. Feeling, intuition, consciousness and spirituality are still banished from the realm of science, notwithstanding some new enlightenment arising from the field of quantum physics. The teaching of conventional economics, which, as incredible as it may sound, claims to be 'value-free', is a conspicuous case in point. A discipline where mathematics has become an end in itself instead of a tool, and where only that which can be measured is important, has generated models and interpretations that are theoretically attractive but totally divorced from reality.

Johannes Brahms composed two concertos for piano and orchestra. Regardless of which of the two may be more to one's liking, it is the first that is fascinating. In fact, it is a splendid exposition of the route Brahms eventually decided not to navigate. We have been left forever with the curiosity of knowing how the *other* Brahms might have been.

That's the way it is. There is a route not navigated, remembered only by 'library worms', and a navigated route to which we attribute spectacular successes and achievements. The universities in particular have chosen the routes of Machiavelli, Bacon, Descartes, Galileo and Newton. As far as St Francis, Pico, Giordano Bruno and Goethe (the scientist) are concerned, they have remained as historical footnotes.

As a result of the navigated route, we have managed to construct a world in which – as suggested by the Catalonian philosopher Jordi Pigem[2] – the Christian virtues such as faith, hope and charity manifest themselves today metamorphosed as schizophrenia, depression and narcissism. The navigation, no doubt, has been fascinating and spectacular. There is much in it to be admired. However, if schizophrenia, depression and narcissism are now the mirror of our existential reality, it is because all of a sudden we find ourselves in a world of confusion. We are in a world of disenchantment, where progress becomes paradoxical and absurd, and reality becomes so incomprehensible, that we desperately seek refuge in a technology that offers us an escape into *virtual realities*.

Where have we arrived?

We have arrived at a point in our human evolution, the characteristic of which is that we *know* a lot, but we *understand* very little. Our chosen navigation has been piloted by reason and leads to the port of knowledge. As such it has been an overwhelmingly successful navigation. We have never in all of our existence accumulated more knowledge than during the last hundred years. We are celebrating the apotheosis of reason, but in the midst of such a splendid celebration we suddenly have the feeling that something is missing.

Yes, we can achieve knowledge about almost anything we want. We can, for instance, guided by our beloved scientific method, study everything there is, from theological, anthropological, sociological, psychological and even biochemical perspectives, about a human phenomenon called *love*. The result will be that we will *know* everything that can be known about love. But once we achieve that complete knowledge, we will sooner or later discover that we will never *understand* love unless we fall in love. We will realize that knowledge is not the road that leads to understanding, because the port of understanding is on another shore and requires a different navigation. We will then be aware that we can attempt to understand only that of which we become a part. That understanding is the result of integration, while knowledge has been the result of detachment. That understanding is holistic, while knowledge is fragmented.

At least we have reached a point at which (many conventional academics notwithstanding) those of us who, in Goethe's perspective, are concerned with the relationship between science and spirituality are finally becoming aware that knowledge is not enough, and that we have to learn how to attain understanding in order to achieve the completeness of our being and the completeness of our science.

We are perhaps beginning to realize that knowledge without understanding is hollow, and understanding without knowledge is incomplete. We therefore need to undertake, at last, the navigation we have so far postponed. But, in order to do so, we must face the great challenge of a language shift.

José Ortega y Gasset, the Spanish philosopher mentioned earlier, used to say that "every generation has its theme". We might add that, in addition, every generation, or historical period, is dominated by, or falls under the spell of, some language. That is the way it is, and there is nothing wrong with it, as long as the dominant language of a given period is coherent with the challenges of that period. The important thing to keep in mind is that language influences our perceptions and hence shapes our actions. Let us look at some examples.

During the first three centuries of the second millennium of Western civilization, the dominant language was of a teleological nature, meaning that human actions had to be justified in terms of a calling that was superior and beyond the needs of everyday life. That made possible the construction of the great cathedrals and monasteries, where time was of no importance. The construction would take 600 years? So what! Nobody was in a hurry. After all, they were constructing for eternity, and eternity is not infinite time, but timelessness. Thank God that the language of 'economic efficiency' had not yet been invented. The importance lay in the deed and not in the time it might take. It was a case of coherence between language and historical challenge.

The language dominating the nineteenth century was basically that of the consolidation of the nation-state. The great speeches of political leaders such as Disraeli, Gladstone and Bismarck are relevant examples. Without going into details, we may also say that the dominant language of the century was coherent with the historical challenge of the times.

It is only in the twentieth century, especially during the second half, that the dominant language is that of economics. A quick overview shows some interesting perspectives. The late 1920s and early 1930s, the time of the so-called great depression, coincides with the emergence of Keynesian economics. The Keynesian language is in many ways the product of a crisis, having the capacity of both interpreting the crisis and overcoming it. It is, again, a language (or rather sub-language) coherent with its historical period.

The next sub-language shift occurs during the 1950s and 1960s, with the emergence of the so-called developmental language. This was an optimistic, utopian and happy language. Economists writing in those days were mainly dominated by the feeling that, at last, we had discovered how to promote true development and overcome world poverty. It is unnecessary to reproduce the prescriptions here, but it should be pointed out that, although the hoped-for goals were not fully achieved, many things during those decades changed in a positive manner. This language was at least partially coherent with its historical challenges.

And then came the last three decades of the twentieth century, with the emergence of the neoliberal discourse. This is a language that still dominates, during a period in which global poverty has increased dramatically, the burden of debt has crippled many national economies and generated the brutal overexploitation of both people and natural resources, the destruction of ecosystems and biodiversity has reached levels unknown in human history, and the accumulation of financial wealth in ever-fewer hands has reached obscene proportions. The disastrous effects of this language, absolutely incoherent with its historical challenges, is clear enough to be seen by everyone, although decision-makers and holders of power prefer to look in the opposite direction and hold on to their pseudo-religious concoction.

Where do we go from here?

There is a tendency in the West to perceive ourselves as members of a successful culture. However, the truth is that no matter how much we extend the concept of success, we are still incomplete beings, materially overdeveloped and spiritually poor. And most probably it is that incompleteness, that poverty, which is responsible for the uneasiness and anxieties that permeate our existence in the world today. Perhaps the moment has arrived in which to rest and reflect. We have the opportunity now to analyse with true honesty the map that shows where we have navigated, with all its hazards and successes; all its tragedies and glories. And then it may be wise to unearth the alternative map of the route we did not navigate, and see whether we can find in it orientations that can rescue us from our existential confusion.

As a consequence of the unearthing of the forgotten map, perhaps it would make sense that we start seeing brothers and sisters surrounding us. Perhaps it would be good to believe in the possibilities of harmony between many possible truths. Perhaps it may be to our advantage that we dare to imagine and believe that the Earth has a soul and that everything is life. Perhaps it would be good to realize that there is no reason whatsoever to banish intuition, spirituality and consciousness from the realm of science. Or, to put it in Goethe's words: "If [we] would seek comfort in the whole, [we] must learn to discover the whole in the smallest part", because "nothing is more consonant with Nature than that she puts into operation in the smallest detail that which she intends as a whole."[3]

Our passionate pursuit of knowledge has postponed our navigation towards understanding. There should be nothing to impede the undertaking of such a navigation now, were it not for an economics which, as practised under the spell of the neoliberal discourse, increasingly distorts reality, thus contributing to our confusion and to the falsification of knowledge itself.

No sustainability (which obviously requires understanding) will or can be achieved without a profound language shift. We need a new language that opens the door of understanding; that is, not a language of power and domination, but a language that may emerge from the depth of our self-discovery as an inseparable part of a whole that is the cradle of the miracle of life. If we manage to provoke such a shift, we may still experience the satisfaction of having brought about a new century worth living in.

Let us hope for a safe voyage and a fulfilling navigation towards the shores that may turn us into complete beings capable of understanding the completeness of life.

Chapter 2

The function of economics in society

In the previous chapter we travelled through the bifurcations of our Western civilization in general. In the chapters ahead we will travel through the bifurcations that have affected the development of the discipline of economics.

We, the authors, hold that economics fulfils a function in society parallel with, and supplementary to, law: namely that of a bulwark of class structure. The class structure of society has always been supported and stabilized by the existing systems of law. This is an important *raison d'être* of all legal codes. The Codex Hammurabi (the oldest well-preserved ancient law code, dating to c.1792 BC in ancient Babylon, which scaled punishments depending on social status, e.g. of slave versus free man) was formulated explicitly to support the class structure and, although in other law systems this function is not explicitly mentioned, it is implicit in the legal codes. As the Western feudal period drew to a close, there appeared the need, in order to maintain stability, for more than a system based on the force of law. The outlines of this development are sketched below.

Justifying the status quo

One may divide the functions of law into protection of (the integrity of) life and limb on the one hand; and protection of privilege, especially (the possession of) property, on the other. The parts of law concerned with the former, and of the collection of customs that prevail in relations between individuals, are almost universally felt to be *natural*, and therefore need no justification. In the feudal period of Western history, the same naturalness was held – by those with authority – to be true of the laws relating to property. Feudal law governed the class structure and was all that was needed to specify societal relationships completely. These relationships were seen and accepted by all, including by the powerless and oppressed, as God-given. In the measure that the power and riches of the trading (and later manufacturing) class – the bourgeoisie[1] – grew, bringing the feudal period to a close, the real, but hidden, conflict between the haves and the have-nots came into the open as a permanent feature of society. Machiavelli was the first to describe this basic dichotomy, using as an example his own city of Florence. In paragraph IX of *The Prince* he distinguishes in every city (i.e. society) two 'dispositions', the *people* and the *powerful*,[2] and "The people are everywhere anxious to not be dominated or oppressed by the powerful, and the powerful are out to dominate and oppress the people." Where his own sympathy lies comes out clearly a few lines later, where he writes: "The people are more honest in their intentions than the powerful because the latter want to oppress the people, whereas the people want only to *not be* oppressed." In Chapter 3 of this book, where we present our own sympathies, it will become apparent that, as far as this ethical point is concerned, we are with Machiavelli.[3]

This basic conflict has been a principal determinant of historical developments in the second half of the second millennium. It has lurked behind all of the revolutions, uprisings and riots that Western society has known. In philosophical and ethical history, the proponents of various utopias have always dreamed of a world in which this conflict is resolved. A good example is Marx's prediction, not based on any precedent or observation but simply 'pulled out of the hat', that the State would 'wither away' once the possession of the means of production was settled in the right way. Following Machiavelli, the political philosopher Claude Lefort sees this and similar trains of thought as empty dreams. In his opinion, if we set our dreams aside and learn from what history teaches us, we must conclude that the conflict between the people (the common man) and the powerful cannot be permanently resolved; it is a never-ending and *indissoluble conflict*. The best that we can do is to provide, in our social and political arrangement, for the possibility that the people may engage in fair battles – i.e. battles governed by fixed rules – in the continuing struggle. As does Lefort, we (the authors) hold that democracy is the only social order that provides, or ever can provide, a platform on which the conflict can be more or less fairly fought out. This platform, with a law-making legislative branch and an independent judiciary next to the executive branch, as described by Montesquieu, can exist only in a democracy where the seat of power is relinquishable and only temporarily occupied by one faction or another. This temporariness makes it impossible (in principle) for an occupant of the seat to bring about a permanent settlement of the conflict. In authoritarian forms of society, the inter-class relationships are (pre)determined by the ruling oligarchy, and thus not open to question. In such a system the judiciary is also subservient to the ruling group or faction.

At the same time that this picture recommends itself to egalitarian thinking, it also pinpoints the vulnerability of democratic government. The powerful are always irritated by democracy; they would prefer to settle the conflict according to their own preferences (and to their advantage, of course). This desire has led the power-hungry, from Julius Caesar onwards, again and again to subvert democracy in order to rid themselves of this irritating platform.

With the rise of the bourgeoisie came a need for a new discipline that would justify their financial power. The 'naturalness' of great riches and the political power these gave to the possessors was no longer apparent because it was no longer credible that this social order was ordained by God. The ways in which the rich became rich and powerful was visible to everyone who had eyes to see, whereas in the feudal period the powerful were born powerful, the powerless were born powerless, and it had been that way as long as anyone could remember. The concept, born in the Renaissance, that everyone was a unique individual, began slowly to do its leavening work, so that in the course of time it became impossible to maintain that some were and some were not born with natural rights to property. The law, in the form of police and militia, could be counted on physically to defend the possessions of the rich from popular anger, which it has been called upon to do many thousands of times in the last 500 years. Physically, then, the powerful were able to dispose as they desired of the wealth created by the people, but since their rights to this disposition lacked the blessing of God, another intellectual foundation was called for. This was especially so since the egalitarian tendencies that gradually manifested themselves after the Renaissance made it less and less certain that the law would always provide that protection. The need for another prop, or buttress, made itself felt. This is particularly urgent in a democracy, where the powerful must always gird themselves for another round in the indissoluble conflict.

Arguments were needed to show that the hunger of the poor is *natural*, and that trying to alleviate it would go against nature and disrupt the orderly state of affairs. Another institution, besides the law, dedicated to maintaining the social order was needed to provide these arguments. It would have to not only formulate the theoretical justification of the new order but also provide instruments to protect the possessors of accumulated wealth from the enactment of laws and regulations that might threaten their right to such possession. It would also have to provide the rationalization of mechanisms (such as an unregulated market) by which the continuous siphoning-off of wealth, and thus power, from its creators (i.e. those who work) to the wealthy could be justified as right and proper.

The birth of economics and its reinvention

To fill this need, the discipline of economics arose. That the social dichotomy was not just the way things *were*, but also the way things *ought to be*, has from the very beginning been the basis of the new economics. By 'new economics' we mean that school of thought which chose the bifurcation that led to the justification of the status quo, since economics has not always been the same.

Let us see what economics was, as originally conceived, compared with what it has become.

Aristotle, in the introductory chapter of his *Politics*,[4] makes a clear distinction between what he calls *oikonomia* (the art of household management) and *krematistiké* (the art of acquisition).

> Aristotle's *oikonomia* included the study and practice of diverse domains related to the (re)production of use-values such as agriculture, crafts, hunting and gathering, mining and even warfare. It included as well the discussion of meaning and value, of ethics and aesthetics, as an integral part of his *'art of living and living well'*. It represented, thus, a use-value-centred approach to the economic process, articulated around the production for self-consumption and the basic aim of improving households' well-being. Commerce (chrematistics) assumed a secondary role therein. Within chrematistics, he further introduced a fundamental distinction between two kinds of

commerce: one subordinated to the use-value logic and thus the *oikonomia* (providing households with the use-value needs which were in short supply internally in exchange for those produced in excess), and another concerned with the 'art of money-making' – accumulation of exchange-values by means of commerce – which he rightly saw as secondary from a logical and historical point of view. Once this latter principle was established as an end in itself – dissociated from the wider use-value logic of the *oikonomia* – this kind of chrematistics was no longer instrumental to the *oikonomia*, and was considered by Aristotle as being external and 'unnatural' to it.[5]

Aristotelian economics, dealing with *the art of living and living well*, valid for all citizens, could certainly not be invoked as a justification for the maintenance of the status quo. However, as a sad bifurcation, chrematistics – if brought to the forefront – would do the trick. Reversing Aristotle's exposition, use-value logic subordinated to exchange-value logic became the foundation of a new economics, from whose language the concept of chrematistics (now called economics) disappeared altogether.

To justify the acquisition of wealth and power, the discipline of the new economics (former chrematistics) arose. In this new light, poverty is supposed to be prescribed by *natural law*,[6] and by reasoning – with an obvious logical gap – it is assumed that when the powerful accumulate wealth, everyone is better off. In his *General Theory* Keynes has identified the twist to reality given by Ricardo to veil, or rationalize away, the misery caused by economic cycles. Ricardo simply declared economic cycles to be impossible, and thereby became the originator of the economic maxim: 'If theory and reality collide, ignore reality.' Keynes explains this as follows.

> The idea that we can safely neglect the aggregate demand function is fundamental to the Ricardian economics, which underlie what we have been taught for more than a century. Malthus, indeed, had vehemently opposed Ricardo's doctrine . . . but vainly. For, since Malthus was unable to explain clearly (apart from an appeal to . . . common observation) how and why effective demand could be deficient or excessive, he failed to furnish an alternative construction; and Ricardo conquered England as completely as the Holy Inquisition conquered Spain. . . .

The completeness of the Ricardian victory is something of a curiosity and a mystery. It must have been due to a complex of suitabilities in the doctrine to the environment into which it was projected. That it reached conclusions quite different from what the ordinary uninstructed person would expect, added I suppose to its intellectual prestige. That its teaching, projected into practice, was austere and often unpalatable, lent it virtue. That it was adapted to carry a vast and consistent logical superstructure, gave it beauty. That it could explain much social injustice and apparent cruelty as an inevitable incident in the scheme of progress, and the attempt to change such things as likely on the whole to do more harm than good, commended it to authority. That it afforded a measure of justification to the free activities of the individual capitalist, attracted to it the support of the dominant social force behind authority.[7]

Adam Smith's magnum opus is called *The Wealth of Nations*, but it is not very clear *whose* wealth he was writing about. Adam Smith was a man with an unusually well-developed social conscience for the age in which he lived, who more than once criticized the cruel and unjust treatment of the working class. Yet in his world view the existence of the class dichotomy was always simply taken for granted as a natural phenomenon. The following quotation is revealing.

A man must live by his work, and his wages must be at least enough to maintain him. They must *even* upon most occasions be somewhat more; otherwise it would be impossible for him to bring up a family, and the *race* of such workmen could not last beyond the first generation.[8] [Our italics.]

In other words, while Smith felt sympathy for badly treated workers, it never entered his head that they might be his equals as human beings. His use of the word *race* may be partly metaphorical, but it seems clear to us that he saw workers as a separate category of beings that had a specific function in the scheme of things, as farm animals do. He felt that they should be treated decently, but the thought that they might have intrinsic human value was far beyond him.

Furthering the intellectual prestige of economics

In order to successfully fulfil the role of defender of the status quo, economics as a discipline had to become, like natural science, intellectually respectable. This is, however one looks at it, a formidable task. We will discuss the way this task was accomplished in Chapter 5, where it will be seen that dressing economics in mathematical robes, a process initiated towards the end of the nineteenth century, played an important role. But still this did not, in itself, give economics the status that was needed to make plausible that economists are *bona fide* academics who deal in objective truth. A giant step in this direction was the creation by the Swedish National Bank in 1969, in the name of Alfred Nobel (he was dead and could not defend himself), of a yearly prize for the 'best' economist(s). The names of the recipients are announced on the anniversary of Nobel's death, just as are the names of the winners of the real Nobel Prizes. There appears to be no impediment to choosing in one year two winners whose economic 'truths' are totally contradictory; nor does the bank seem to be embarrassed if winners turn out to be criminals.

In this respect, it is interesting to quote the historian of science Yves Gingras, who relates the incident at the award ceremonies for 1970 as follows.

> Paul Samuelson [1970 winner] wrote about his 'Nobel coronation' – not his 'Bank of Sweden coronation' – and filled his talk with references to Einstein (4 times), Bohr (2 times) and eight other winners of the (real) physics Nobel prize (not to mention, of course, Newton) plus a few other names as if he were part of this family.[9]

Furthermore, as pointed out by Edward Fullbrook:

> For the last 50 years economics as a profession has shown exceptional talent for self-promotion. Spurred on by self-delusion, it has persuaded the media to call its Bank of Sweden Prize a 'Nobel Prize' and in the main has escaped ridicule when – like Samuelson and others – it has represented its pursuits and achievements as resembling those of Newton and Einstein. This self-exaltation has in the main enabled its anti-scientific methodology to escape outside notice, with the result that the broader intellectual community has accepted economics' self-assessment.[10]

The great divide

Although they worked in concert at the common task of rationalizing the existence of poverty on the one hand and immense wealth on the other as natural phenomena, practitioners of the new profession had quite divergent views of what the 'correct' international financial order would look like. These views depended on which policies would most favour their local ruling class. In the early days of capitalism, as pointed out by J. K. Galbraith, this deferential attitude led American and German economists to postulate quite different absolute truths from those of their British counterpart, Adam Smith. The difference concerned the best trade policy for a nation. Whereas the former supported autarky – necessary, in a small, undeveloped economy, to protect its own 'infant industries' against foreign competition – the latter supported free trade – favourable for the powerful British economy that needed the opposite: wide-open external markets. This core difference, obviously dependent on whose financial advantage the policies serve, does not seem to embarrass economists. Nor does it even bring them to doubt their claim to the same professional status as natural scientists. Moreover, as indicative of the weak intellectual status of economic thought as this glossing-over of such deep-lying differences in 'eternal truths' is, it is, in our view, not the most important shortcoming in the profession. We see the question of social justice as the most important disagreement between 'mainstream' economists and 'others'. Social justice plays no part in the thinking of the former, but is the sine qua non of a well-functioning economic system for the latter.

And this is what this whole book is about. We argued earlier in this chapter that economics arose, as did law, as a mechanism of protection of the class structure of society. This became necessary as an additional buttress to wealth and power once the word of God no longer sufficed to keep the populace in line. Nonetheless, there have always been dissidents. Hailing back to the 'indissoluble conflict' at the foundation of society, we label economists according to which side of the conflict they choose to stand on. Those generally denoted as 'mainstream' occupy themselves with the defence of the 'rights' and privileges of the powerful; the possessors of accumulated wealth; Machiavelli's nobili. It is notable that they seem quite unaware of this function. This lack of awareness, or perhaps it is repression, is part and parcel of the subject of value premises, which we address in detail in Chapter 4. It also appears crystal clear in the arguments used by von Hayek against social justice, which are discussed in Chapter 3.

There are, however, quite a few economists who look at things differently and take a basically different approach to economic problems. In the early nineteenth century the very human Jean Charles Léonard de Sismondi proposed the same kind of governmental intervention as John Maynard Keynes (actually much broader, in the direction of the welfare state – a direction not followed by Keynes), when necessary to restore the balance to the supply-and-demand equilibrium if the market becomes glutted. His goal, and perhaps Keynes's goal too, was to protect the working classes from being driven into destitution. He deviated from the ideas of Adam Smith by placing himself firmly against the laissez-faire principles of Ricardo. His humanly inspiring ideas of how an economic system should function made (and today still make) no impression on the mainstream, which accepts human suffering as a – perhaps somewhat unfortunate – by-product of a well-functioning economy. It is never stated this way in academic circles, but the thesis of this book is that in the dominant world view the real goal of a well-functioning economic system is to protect the wealth and power of the rich.

It may be noted that economics is not the only discipline in which some of its practitioners defend the correctness and inevitability of the division of society into the powerless poor and powerful rich. Some sociologists have also played a supporting role in the game, substituting the tenets of social Darwinism for the authority that God's word had under feudalism (with approximately equal intellectual validity). In their world view, evolution, stretching over several billion years, is imagined to apply equally to human society on a time scale commensurate with human life, leading to the 'evolution' of millionaires as the flower of mankind. George Graham Sumner of Yale University was one of the foremost representatives of this school of thought, fashionable in reactionary circles.

Chapter 3

Keynesianism: its rise and fall

In the aftermath of the 1929 crash it was impossible for anyone, economist or not, to persist in the Ricardian absurdity that demand could never be deficient. The trauma caused by the crash did not subside for a generation, and Keynes's solution to insufficient demand, through a strong State intervention and public works, was accepted by a majority of the economics profession and even became part of economic education. In order to understand the historical picture, one must note that in the same period two other historically unique occurrences brought about an upheaval, both physical and spiritual, in Western society. These were, firstly, the two world wars, and, secondly, the birth of the Soviet Union. For the first time in history, the political leaders of Western democracies had to mobilize the entire population, so that the wars became people's wars. In order to achieve this in democratically governed nations, they were forced to espouse all manner of egalitarian principles, whether or not they had the intention of ever translating these into realities. Those who lived through these periods will not forget how thick and fast the words 'democracy', 'liberty' and 'freedom' flew through the air.

But if the ruling elite, with all their lip-service to democracy and freedom, had no intention of creating a more just society, the people, having been hooked into ghastly bloodletting, did not forget these principles when it was over. This was an important factor in the post-war popular movements, and explains why the British threw out their great wartime leader, Winston Churchill, at the very first opportunity. But if it hadn't been for the threat to capitalism embodied in the very existence of the Soviet Union, the centres of power would not have had to grant such far-reaching concessions to social justice as were achieved through social security and a substantial socialisation of medicine, alongside greatly increased governmental interference in the working of the economic system. The same social leavening was also, of course, at work in bringing about the (also historically unique) period of decolonization. There was so much going on at the same time – including, after the Second World War, the most insane arms race in history – that it is not easy to construct a valid, broad, picture of the whole. The disparity between socialist dreams of a just society and the reality of Soviet society was certainly real and important. But of greater political importance is the fact that the very existence of Soviet society awoke dreams of a just world – dreams that have lived on, sometimes slumbering, in the hearts and minds of millions.

However complex the picture and the motivations may have been, the simultaneous ascendancy of Keynesian economics and a previously unknown level of social justice were perhaps initially coincidental, but they were certainly mutually reinforcing. And although the majority of economists were (temporarily) won over to governmental involvement in the functioning of the economy, the ranks were already forming for the battle against the welfare state and Keynesian economics. Both before and after the Second World War (and, in fact, right up to the present) the London School of Economics (LSE) was the pied-à-terre of the die-hard (economic) liberals. At the same time a lesser-known institute, the Institute of Economic Affairs (IEA) provided a well-financed (by a wealthy chicken farmer) workplace to plan and carry out practical strategies.

In fact, the movement to get the wealth-producing sectors of the population back into the harness, and divest them of political power, began between the two world wars, many years before the outside world became aware of it. The *nobili* were gathering strength for the coming battle in the 'indissoluble conflict'. A little-noticed meeting took place in Paris in 1938, attended by a number of academics opposed to the growing spirit of social welfare (called collectivism or *étatisme* by its enemies). It was named Le Colloque Walter Lippmann by the organizer, the French academic Louis Rougier, in honour of the American columnist whose anti-New-Deal writings had attracted attention on the other side of the Atlantic. He attended the meeting himself, and the Austrian economists Friedrich von Hayek and Ludwig von Mises also participated. The first of these was to become the foremost crusader after the Second World War for a return to (economic) liberalism. In the closing period of the Second World War, von Hayek's broadside against State involvement in the economic life of the nation, *The Road to Serfdom*,[1] formed a powerful rallying point. He was completely against social security, in particular the proposals of the Beveridge Report, and claimed that the policies of the British Labour Party were essentially the same as those of Adolf Hitler.[2] This position attracted enthusiastic support – and funding – from conservative and business circles. He (as did Orwell in his novel *1984*) predicted in *The Road to Serfdom* that these policies would lead to a crushing dictatorship.

In von Hayek's book he reconstructs the history of Germany in a most remarkable way. He saw no sharp break between the Weimar Republic and the Chancellorship of Adolf Hitler. He even went so far as to say that under the Weimar Republic a completely controlled socialist state had come into existence, so that Hitler's regime only marginally changed the character of the German government. He concentrated completely on the economic control of Germany by Hitler and was not interested in the world-domination dreams of a megalomaniac, nor the horrors of a totalitarian state based on terror. The exercise was directed entirely towards proving that it is inevitable that once the government gets involved in the economic life of a nation a crushing dictatorship will emerge. In his choice of arguments, a number of elements emerge which, we believe, prove that his real concern was with the maintenance of the existing power structure. We return to this point below.

The birth of the Mont Pelerin Society

When the war was over, in order to renew the initiative begun so many years before in the Colloque Walter Lippmann, von Hayek gathered a group of like-minded persons to discuss the issues – in his eyes, the dangers – of the welfare state. It was named the Mont Pelerin Society (MPS) after its meeting place on the slopes of Mont Pèlerin overlooking Lac Léman in Switzerland. The first meeting took place in November 1947. Most of the participants were economists, but other academics who were staunch economic liberals, such as Karl Popper and Michael Polanyi, also took part.

The ideology of the MPS

It is important to look critically at the arguments used by von Hayek in his crusade to restore his brand of freedom to the English people. He was always very careful in his choice of words, in a way that today would be called 'politically correct'. In particular he never stops prizing the English liberal tradition. To appear more British he even left the 'von' out of his name. We discuss here several of the key words, or slogans, of his crusade.

Labour (unions)

A good example is the contrast between von Hayek's words in *The Road to Serfdom* about trade unions and the fact that trade union power was one of the primary targets for destruction for those gathered in the MPS. In the book he describes the trade union as a "great democratic movement" that went wrong when it began to strive for the right to collective bargaining. He saw this as a collectivist trick to reduce the worker to slavery.

> The fatal turning point in the modern development was when the great movement which can serve its original end only by fighting all privilege, the labour movement, came under the influence of anti-competition doctrines and became itself entangled in the strife for privilege. . . . It is one of the saddest spectacles of our time to see a great democratic movement support a policy which must lead to the destruction of democracy and which meanwhile can benefit only a minority of the masses who support it. . . . So long as labour continues to assist in the destruction of the only order under which at least some degree of independence and freedom has been secured to *every worker*, there is indeed little hope for the future.[3]

You can almost hear him sobbing in pity at the plight of the worker who was reduced to the slavery, for the first time in history, of having something to say about his own working conditions. His picture of the "degree of independence and freedom" that every worker enjoys has little in common with the reality of the life of the worker before trade union power provided him with some protection, who knew only that he must do what he is told, or go hungry. That he had little insight into his own motivations is demonstrated by the fact that von Hayek himself enjoyed very great privileges, yet wrote as if the desire for privilege is something unworthy. Just like Adam Smith, he saw the worker as another sort of being. The privileges that he himself enjoyed were in his eyes inconceivable in the life of a worker.

In his opening speech to the MPS, von Hayek used quite different wording. Here the trade union was no longer a "great democratic movement" but had become an organization given to "violence, coercion and intimidation".

> We must not delude ourselves that in many ways the most crucial, the most difficult and delicate part of our task consists in formulating an appropriate programme of Labour or trade union policy. In no other respect, I believe, was the development of liberal opinion more inconsistent or more unfortunate or is there more vagueness even among the true liberals of today. Historically liberalism first for too long maintained an unjustified opposition against trade unions as such, only to collapse completely by the beginning of this century and to grant to trade unions in many respects exemption from the ordinary law and even, to all intents and purposes, to *legalise violence, coercion and intimidation*. That if there is to be any hope of a return to a free economy the question how the powers of trade unions can be appropriately delimited in law as well as in fact is one of the most important of all the questions to which we must give our attention.[4]

As is well known, under Margaret Thatcher's regime the powers of the trade unions were indeed, to the satisfaction of economic liberals, 'appropriately delimited', i.e. destroyed. The worker became again what he had always been, powerless to defend his dignity and his livelihood. But here the important message is von Hayek's Janus-face.

Unemployment versus full employment

Unemployment has always been an important weapon of the powerful to keep workers in line. That is why every programme of social reform since the beginning of the industrial revolution has had full employment as an important slogan. It stood high on the Labour agenda during the Second World War. In their opposition to this, von Hayek and the Tories were again careful not to mention the power element, and even more careful to avoid giving the impression that cheap labour was the real goal, but based their public opposition on the supposed danger of inflation if full employment were to become a reality. That 'too' high employment must lead to inflation is a fundamental postulate of mainstream economic theory. That this is not based on empirical

evidence is apparently no more a reason to doubt it than to doubt other postulates of economic theory that lack empirical foundation. The fact is that in
the 25 or so years of the post-war so-called 'Days of Hope', both unemployment *and* inflation were quite low in the Western capitalist countries. The
actual relationship from a historical perspective is a complicated matter that
we cannot go into here (an excellent analysis covering the post-war years can
be found in Ormerod[5]). We mention it here only to show that the (publicly)
expressed reason of economic liberals for opposition to full employment had
no basis in fact, obliging one to enquire into the possibility that quite different
motives were behind it.

We suggest that one motive is the role that subjecting the worker to discipline
plays in the world view of the economic liberal. In *The Road to Serfdom* von
Hayek explains the problem (and its solution) as follows.

> The application of the engineering technique to a whole nation – and
> this is what planning means – 'raises problems of discipline which
> are hard to solve', as has been well described by an American engi-
> neer[6] with great experience in government planning, who has clearly
> seen the problem.

> 'In order to do an engineering job,' he explains, 'there ought to be sur-
> rounding the work a comparatively large area of unplanned economic
> action. There should be a place from which workers can be drawn, and
> when a worker is fired he should vanish from the job and from the pay-
> roll. In the absence of such a free reservoir discipline cannot be main-
> tained without corporal punishment, as with slave labour'.[7]

In this quote we see the true face of the economic liberal. The worker is not a
human with needs and aspirations, but an instrument needed "to do an engineering job" and to be disposed of when not, or no longer, needed. Compare
von Hayek's approval of this attitude here and his remarks later in the same
book, quoted on page 33. It goes without saying that with full employment the
situation described in the above quote cannot be realized, which partly
explains the opposition of the economic liberal to full employment.

The other motive, referred to above, is that if the power of the community of workers is broken, wages can be kept low. Exactly how low was stated precisely in the quote in Chapter 2 (see page 26) from Adam Smith's *The Wealth of Nations*.

The rule of law

In *The Road to Serfdom* von Hayek spends many words in explaining why the rule of law would have to die if a government-controlled economic system were to come into being. One is struck by his oft-repeated statement that the most important positive aspect of the rule of law is that it takes the shape of *formal rules* that can be made in advance, and "do not aim at the wants and needs of particular people. . . . And they are, or ought to be, intended for such long periods that it is impossible to know whether they will assist particular people more than others." What he does not say is that although the rule of law does not aim at *particular people*, it most certainly aims at *particular classes of people* and as such has an unexpressed goal of preserving class distinctions (and privileges). In that respect he shares the conviction of all mainstream economists that class struggle doesn't exist. So, although he is quite right in saying that the law does not protect certain pre-specified persons, it is no accident that those whom the law protects have in common that they possess some measure of wealth (in one form or another). This is not the place to enter into the moral and ethical issues involved in possession. It is mentioned only to clarify that von Hayek's arguments on the subject leave out an essential element, probably intentionally.

Free trade

The two interlocking slogans of von Hayek's crusade were 'freedom' and 'competition'. The hallmark of both is *free trade*. It is instructive to compare von Hayek's condemnation of Friedrich List's explanation of the doctrine of free trade with J. K. Galbraith's interpretation of the same. In *The Road to Serfdom* von Hayek writes the following about the ideas of E. H. Carr.

> He even takes over the German thesis, originated by Friedrich List, that free trade was a policy dictated solely by, and appropriate only to, the special interests of England in the nineteenth century.[8]

It is a fair question to ask whether List's view vis-à-vis free trade, ridiculed by von Hayek, is so obviously wrong. Galbraith sees the issue through rational lenses, and judges List's stance quite differently.

> In Britain in the age of industrial triumph nothing was more helpful than the support given by all accepted economic theory to free trade. This was urged both eloquently and elegantly by Adam Smith. Here the accommodation was especially clear. For Britain, the industrially most advanced of countries, free trade was of obvious advantage, and, like laissez faire, it acquired a strong theological aura. In Germany and the United States, on the other hand, economic interest was better served by tariffs. Accordingly, the most respected economists in those countries – the noted Friedrich List in Germany, the eloquent Henry Carey in the United States – spoke vigorously for protection for their national 'infant industries'; protection, in fact, from the products of the British colossus. Such was the service of economics to early capitalism. And such service has continued.[9]

The last sentence in this quotation is confirmed by the twenty-first-century statement of the British New Labour Party's Trade Secretary, Patricia Hewitt: "We want to open up protected markets in developing countries." Hewitt obtained her bachelor's and master's degrees in economics at the University of Cambridge. The basic goal of the discipline of economics in the United Kingdom has clearly not changed over the centuries, nor has it depended on the political allegiances of economists. The question as to whether von Hayek was aware of the deeper motivation behind his attack on List remains debatable. The problem of recognizing what moves one's own inner self, and the role this recognition plays in the social sciences, is treated in Chapter 4.

Social security and freedom

Both the Tories and von Hayek made much of the threat to freedom of the proposed social security proposals of Lord William Beveridge. Richard Cockett, in his history of this epoch, *Thinking the Unthinkable*, discusses, and partly quotes from, a confidential internal report of the Conservative Party on the Beveridge proposals, prepared by an ad hoc committee under the chairmanship of Ralph Assheton:

... Assheton and his colleagues attacked the Beveridge Report with a frankness which was sadly lacking in the public debate on the subject. The Committee took issue with Beveridge on two main points. In the first instance, they argued that Beveridge's proposals were just too expensive, that the country's priority after the war should be to revive her shrunken export trade rather than to embark on an expensive and apparently open-ended scheme of comprehensive social provision in what were bound to be straitened financial circumstances. 'The whole scheme is one for sharing prosperity and if there is no sufficient prosperity to share, it fails.' In the second instance the Committee heavily criticized the implicit 'universality' of Beveridge's Scheme, the idea behind the phrase 'social security' that *everyone* should contribute, via taxation, to the Scheme and that everyone should benefit from it, regardless of *want*. This lack of targeting on those in genuine need was seen not only as extravagant, but also as avowedly redistributionist in its effect; as the Committee pointed out, 'the Scheme becomes more and more one for distributing national income'. The Committee made its objections to both the economic and moral implications of the Beveridge Report very clear:

'It must be realized at once that a great part of the money required for putting his scheme into effect is not devoted to curing want. Sir William (Beveridge) is in search of a comprehensive and unified Scheme of Social Security for the citizens of this country. Provision by the State of complete Social Security can only be achieved at the expense of personal freedom and by sacrificing the right of an individual to choose what life he wishes to lead and what occupation he should follow.'[10]

Let us be very clear about this: of course the plans of Beveridge were redistributionist; no social reform movement worth the name could be otherwise in a land with great differences between rich and poor. The plans were most certainly not a 'scheme for sharing prosperity', but of assuring that what there is, how little or how much, will be shared equitably. They were directed toward the goal of greater social equality, with the accent on removing the terrible uncertainty that every worker lives with: will he be able to provide tomorrow for himself and his family – an uncertainty forever lurking in the minds of the working population. And it is of course that uncertainty that is the wellspring of Tory opposition. The powerful have always been able to exploit it as a weapon of power; a weapon that they most certainly did not wish to lose. It is understandable that they didn't state their opposition in that way. But one still wonders if they couldn't have found a more plausible-sounding objection. Upon reading it, almost 60 years later, it is difficult to realize that it is not meant facetiously. How could the provision of a secure old age to everyone oblige anyone to follow an occupation other than which he or she wished to?

One can add that a good part of the population of an industrial state – the low-income group – has never had much choice in choosing an occupation. The members of the Conservative party elite, quoted above, have no knowledge of (or interest in, for that matter) the stultifying drudgery of the tasks performed, whether willingly or unwillingly, by this very large number of citizens in order to just stay alive.

We find it very difficult to comment in a sober manner on the statements of thinkers such as von Hayek and Popper. When someone sees a great similarity, almost an identity, between the programmes of the British Labour Party and Adolf Hitler's National Socialists, my first reaction is that they must be either joking or insane. But they were deadly serious, and apparently quite unaware of their own deeper-lying class prejudice. It is hard to conclude anything other than that they simply did not want social justice. Popper stated explicitly that if one has to choose between freedom and equality, one must choose freedom. We see no indication, 60 years later, that anyone's freedom has been curtailed by the increased measure of equality brought about by social security, except perhaps if freedom is interpreted to mean the freedom to amass unlimited wealth (not that even that was severely curtailed). We further see, rather than ethical incompatibility, an essential concordance between freedom and equality: for no one in a community can be really free where great inequality prevails.

Competition

Von Hayek, as does every right-thinking economic liberal, places competition at the centre of his value system. And its destruction in a (theoretical) socialist state is, amongst all the bad things in such a state, perhaps the worst. Yet, to his credit, he recognized that if a free-market economy is left to its own devices, competition will equally well be destroyed. Therefore he saw a very clear need for steadfast governmental intervention to prevent this happening, and hence his denial that the ideal economic system is a laissez-faire economy. Measures guaranteeing that competition can do its work are an absolute necessity and belong to the core of liberal economic thought; whether they also belong to its practice is open to serious doubt. To cite an example: why is it that exactly in the last quarter of the twentieth century, when the neoliberal ideals have been applied in practice as seldom before in history, the concentration of economic power (despite the milksop rules meant to prevent it) is progressively eliminating competition so effectively? The reason is not difficult to find: the much-vaunted separation of economics and politics in a liberal society is an illusion. Laws (in this case, laws designed to guarantee free competition) are not made on Olympus but in the nitty-gritty of daily life, where economic power is in no way independent of political power, but rather synonymous with it. Those whose competition-destroying tendencies are supposed to be reined in are closely connected, politically, with those who make and administer the laws that are supposed to suppress these tendencies and prevent them from destroying competition. Is it then a wonder that the necessary laws are either not made, or, if made, are so administered as to benefit economic power above all else?

In the last three decades it is not so much that the strict laws deemed essential by von Hayek have been repealed, or not made, but rather that the judiciary and/or the executive powers have nullified their application in practice. It says a great deal that 90 years after the greatest victory of the Sherman Anti-Trust Act in the United States (we disregard here the legitimate doubts as to whether that Act actually did what it was designed to do), the forced break-up of Standard Oil, the biggest oil companies quietly recombined, while the judiciary, apparently under instructions of the executive,[11] said and did nothing. But the judiciary was not the only sector that remained silent. There is good reason to question whether or not the support by economists of laws to guarantee competition is just empty rhetoric. There was, in any case, no outcry of mainstream economists – not even a whisper – when this milepost fell, and the largest corporation on Earth was reconstituted.

The subject of competition lies at the roots of the thinking of the economic liberal – at the wellspring of the philosophy of liberalism. Competition, when unleashed from its counterweight, cooperation, is basically a violent mode of behaviour. Left on its own, competition will escalate into destructive, all-out conflict. "Hence, those who see virtue in competition must recognize that it is nothing if not *contained* conflict, that it can be sustained only within a moral, societal, and governmental context which ensures that conflicts remain confined with prescribed limits."[12]

We would go one step further and note that the greatest enthusiasts for competition, including well-regulated competition, are those who are powerful and who will certainly win out in 'free' competition. In the Introduction to this book we defined a just world as a world where *all may live in dignity, without fear and with adequate means for satisfying the universal needs of humankind.* The competition ethics of the economic liberal, which glorify predatory behaviour, are diametrically opposed to this view of justice. Civilization is based on working together, on cooperation to reach common goals, competing to see who can contribute the most toward this. Community is the keyword of civilization. The philosophy of the economic liberal, explicitly worded by Margaret Thatcher and echoing Jeremy Bentham, that 'Community doesn't exist', harks back to pre-civilized societies.

We must be clear about this, though. It goes without saying that competition is a normal part of human behaviour and, when counterbalanced with cooperation, is a necessary stimulus for improvement in humanity's lot. The problem arises when competition takes on an ideological dimension; at that point it becomes destructive of human values.

Von Hayek, by painting the picture of a more socially oriented, civilized, society, avoids confronting the fact that his picture of the world is purely instrumental, totally lacking in any human feeling. His ideal world is a cruel world. Some would say that 'the law of the jungle' rules in his society. This is a bad analogy, since in the jungle no animal takes more than it needs. But the analogy is not entirely wrong: in his world the 'other' is not a living, feeling, person, but an instrument for obtaining one's own advantage.

A broad analysis of what competition is, when carried to the extreme of an ideology, has been presented by a group of scholars, The Lisbon Group. They spell out what the ideal world of von Hayek, a world ruled exclusively by competitive behaviour, really means to the people who inhabit this planet.

> Despite its popularity, competitiveness is far from being an effective answer to the present problems and opportunities of the new global world and society. Excess competition is even a source of adverse effects. The most striking result of the competition ideology is that it generates a structural distortion in the functioning of the economy itself, not to mention its devastating social effects.

> First, it has become increasingly evident to many Americans that 'the international economic competition of the past decade[13] has proved a competition in terminating jobs and reducing living standards. Europeans are only now beginning to realize that the search for international competitiveness is being conducted at an unacceptable human cost.'[14] Productive economic competition comes from technological improvement and rationalized industry. Increasing the number of jobless is not the way for a country to grow richer. Nor is impoverishing those with jobs by cutting wages and benefits a socially acceptable form of productivity increase.

> The first result of the competitive war ideology is that the 'North Americans, Europeans and Japanese are all competing by sacrificing the interests of the most vulnerable people in their societies.'[15] Recently, a supporter of the ideology of competitiveness expressed the same idea in a different way. He questioned how British firms could be competitive vis-à-vis South Korea, Indonesia, or China if social protection in Europe were not further reduced and wages remained thirty, forty, or fifty times higher than those in the Asian countries. As we have seen in the previous chapter, the answer given by economic and political leaders has been to favor the reduction of social protection and real wages. How is it possible, however, to believe that there is a reasonable solution to competition between one country in which the average person works 2,200 hours per year for $1,000 and another in which individuals work 1,600 hours for $30,000? Under these conditions, it

is simply demagoguery to claim that the competitiveness of the latter will be increased by a reduction in labor costs.

The second result is that if everyone is competing against everyone else, the value of competitiveness is ultimately lost. As Emile Van Lennep, the former secretary general of the OECD [Organisation for Economic Co-operation and Development], correctly pointed out a decade ago in rejecting competitiveness as the only solution, 'against whom should the OECD as a whole be more competitive? Against the developing world? Against the moon?'[16] 'We cannot', Samuel Brittan argues today, 'all be competitive against each other.'[17] If everyone competes against each other, sooner or later the system will collapse. To survive, the system needs a diverse multiplicity of players. The logic of competitiveness leads to reducing diversity within the system by eliminating all those who are unable to resist the dominant forces. In this sense, it contributes to the development of social exclusion: the noncompetitive people, firms, cities, and nations are left behind. They are no longer the subject of history.

The third effect of the ideology of competitiveness is that it is blinkered. It sees only one dimension of human and social history, that is, the spirit of competition. The spirit of competition and aggression is a powerful engine for action, motivation, and innovation. It does not, however, act in isolation nor is it disconnected from other engines such as the spirit of cooperation and solidarity. Cooperation is also a fundamental phenomenon in human history, produced and determined by society. Competition and cooperation as well as aggressiveness and solidarity are two coexisting, very often conflicting, dimensions of the human condition. The ideology of competitiveness either ignores or devalues cooperation, or it instrumentalizes it to its own logic, as is the case in the great majority of interfirm strategic alliances.

The fourth result is reductionism and sectarian fundamentalism. The ideology of competitiveness not only has just one eye, but it is a bad eye. It does not view at the right scale even the limited things it does see. Competitiveness reduces the entire process of the human condition to the perceptions, motivations, and behavior of *Homo economicus* as *Homo competitor*. All the perceptions, motivations, and behaviors either have no value – unless they are subordinated and legitimized by competitiveness – or they are irrelevant for the economy. The typical magic formula of the ideology of economically dominated competitiveness is 'Let's get back to business.' This formula assumes that when people get back to business, they only talk or do the correct, relevant things.

The ideology of competitiveness does not acknowledge that the market is not the only thing that determines economic development and social well-being. Though the free market has prevailed in the late 1980s, there is no certainty that the market system can cope with the extraordinary tensions that result from the acceleration of, for instance, population growth and environmental degradation. Most marketing feelers are focused on the wealthiest top billion. The market is mostly blind to the aspirations of several billion less wealthy people.

The issue is not to oppose market and nonmarket forces and argue about what is more important. The argument is that both are critical and that it is the balanced relations between them that are of paramount importance. The more the ideology of competitiveness fails to see everything and sees inadequately what it does, the more it claims that what it sees is the exclusive ultimate reality. Competitiveness fundamentalists are aggressive in their theory, blind in their approach, and sectarian in their judgment. Ultimately they can become arrogant.[18]

Deregulation and privatization

As already remarked, von Hayek was definitely a supporter of enforcing laws that guarantee that competition is fair. Strict rules for accounting are, of course, an absolute necessity, since competition cannot work unless the true facts concerning the functioning of all businesses are known to all. Unfortunately for the stability of the present system, a new spirit has taken a hold of the business world since the late 1970s. That spirit is called deregulation, and the most important victims are regulations that impose some modicum of decency on the accounting practices of corporations. There is no reason to doubt that mainstream economists, *in principle*, are in favour of such regulations, but recent history gives us good reason to doubt that they are willing to go out on a limb and fight for them, especially when their benefactors are pushing to get rid of them. After all, it was Alan Greenspan, the former Chairman of the US Federal Reserve and thoroughbred economic liberal who, using his political power as boss of the Fed, was instrumental in the softening of the regulations of accountants' practices and thus opened the floodgates for the Enron disaster, and others.

But to leave it at that would be to ignore the deeper meaning of government regulation of business practices, and to speak only of the most visible egregious consequences of deregulation. Human beings, physically rather weak animals, have become masters of this planet by learning to work together for the common good. In this process we have evolved to what we are, a social animal. Communities were (and are) sometimes organized in very unpleasant ways, but what is essential is that without the cooperation, forced or voluntary, of practically all members of every community, we would all not be here now. Over the course of time in Western society the function of government grew towards an adulthood in which the general welfare of the community became its responsibility. The obvious consequence is that behaviour deleterious to the common good must be monitored and prevented, and, in particular, the weaker members of society, who cannot fend so well for themselves, must be protected.

And there lies the rub. Using the slogan of the free market, neoliberal economists promote the belief that government regulation is to everybody's disadvantage, because it inhibits competition. The argument is logically untenable, since the fundamental doctrine of liberal economics demands that the government actively defend competition by regulations that prevent its destruction by the natural working of the market. Logically, then, one would have to choose between, on the one hand, accepting the destruction of competition by the unregulated market, or on the other, the defence of competition by regulating the market. By slurring over this distinction with a great deal of brouhaha about 'how a free market means competition, and thus lower prices', the not-all-too-logically-thinking neoliberal provides himself with an effective selling point for government policy that leads directly to disasters (which only hit the little guys) such as the aforementioned Enron affair. But this is not really enough for the dyed-in-the-wool neoliberal. It would be even better to get rid of the government entirely.

Privatization is therefore the next step in divesting government of the responsibility for the welfare of the whole. The idea behind this is that government is, in principle, inefficient, and that in private hands the drive toward profit will bring about efficiency automatically. Here we have used the word 'efficiency' in its bare, instrumental sense. Applied in practice this means that efficient railroads would no longer have stations in out-of-the-way towns, and the post would no longer be delivered to outlying districts. Used in this way, the word 'efficiency' makes a mockery of the idea of the 'whole'. One could play innocent of the ways of the world and say that it is for our societies to decide what they want. Do we want the exclusion of the weak, those who are different – or do we want the inclusion of all of us in the whole? *Vox populi* must decide. But this would be naive. In this period of history, this decision has unfortunately been pre-empted by the powerful. *Vox populi* is a very quiet little voice now, just as it was in the world of Machiavelli.

The question is not whether everything should be decided by the government or whether everything should be placed in the hands of a ruling elite. I (Philip) am enough of a Pollyanna to believe that there is an intermediate position, simply described as a regime in which those sectors that take care of providing services *that we all need* are the responsibility of the government, whereas all other sectors are left to private initiative. Surely this is not inherently unreasonable.

The unravelling of Keynesianism

Although the concentrated campaign of von Hayek and his kindred spirits was of great importance in the process, one should not forget the role of time itself. In the Second World War years and in those just before and just after, thousands of idealistic, community-minded people entered government service in the capitalist countries. This flood of humanistic thinking was fundamental in bringing about the leavening of society described at the beginning of this chapter. But everything changes with time. As the 1960s and 1970s wore on, death and retirement took their toll, and the ranks of the stout defenders of a more human world were slowly decimated, and finally reduced to an ineffective level.

In the meantime, in England the Institute of Economic Affairs (IEA) – von Hayek's pied-à-terre – and, later, the 'Selsdon Group' of economic liberals on the fringe of the Conservative Party, were churning out publications. These were intended to convince politicians and the public that deregulation and privatization would return the economy to its rightful course, i.e. endless growth with a chastened and disciplined low-wage labour force. The publications must have played a role in re-educating non-members of the parish, but it is impossible to know how large a role it was.

In the 1970s the picture changed further, with the appearance in the industrialized countries of simultaneous stagnation of economic growth and inflation, i.e. *stagflation*. This has afflicted the poor countries since time immemorial; however, economists treated it as if it were a new phenomenon and gave it a name when it hit at home. The oil shocks that came along at about the same time as the stagflation make the overall picture murky; cause and effect can hardly be proven.

But the argument was made that Keynesian demand management simply didn't work any more. That other causes (besides the failure of Keynesian policies) could be at work was not even considered by von Hayek, the Conservative Party, the Selsdon Group or the IEA. But whatever the causes may have been, it is perverse to postulate that free markets, no governmental intervention and powerless trade unions – a formula tried for one-and-a-half centuries and leading, with mathematical certainty, to recurrent collapse and social devastation – were needed to cure the disease.

The point is that much more was at stake than just an economic theory. The concept of the welfare state was inextricably woven into the patterns of Keynesian thinking (somewhat more into the thinking of Keynesians than in the thinking of Keynes). And that concept was the real enemy. The ideas of the new supply-side economics, as exemplified by the thoughts of von Hayek and the MPS, were the weapons of the ruling class in the much broader context of the 'indissoluble conflict'.

However, there was still, 30 years after the war, the lingering dream of a more just world standing in the way of total victory for von Hayek. Irrespective of whether or not the socialism of the Soviet Union and its satellites was a humanly acceptable approximation to a just society, the socialist dream of a world in which everyone had his or her say and could live in dignity would not, and will not, die. The self-dubbed 'libertarians', who by using this term usurped the name of liberty to describe their economic liberalism, hold forth a picture of *social capitalism* in which universal ownership, through share-holding, empowered the entire population. We quote an example from a recent well-documented study of 'the miracle of the market'.

Every historical movement to rein in Wall Street; every argument for regulating or otherwise controlling American business has taken as its starting point the imperatives of democracy. Financial practices, reformers have charged again and again, stand in flagrant violation of our common values of justice, equality, and universal representation. In the nineties, though, the narrative of populist Wall Street seemed to prove the exact opposite: popular *participation* in the stock market amounted to popular *sanction* of both the processes of the exchange and the corporations whose shares were traded. When pundits spoke of the stock market having been 'democratized', they implied that the market now functioned like a democracy; that the market represented the people, that it acted on the people's behalf, that it spoke in the *Vox Populi*. Markets were not merely organs of exchange, they were a never-ending election that had, in Thomas Friedman's phrase, 'turned the whole world into a parliamentary system', a place where people 'vote every hour, every day through their mutual funds, their pension funds, their brokers, and, more and more, from their own basements via the internet.'[19] The NYSE [New York Stock Exchange], once the locus of elite power, had become a national town meeting, its daily tickings up or down as much an expression of the people's will as of economic well-being. The bull market of the nineties was to be nothing less than the People's Market, a combination of voting booth and prosperity machine for the common man.

So just as efficient market theory holds that stock markets process economic data quickly and flawlessly, American commentators came to believe that stock markets perform pretty much the same operation with the general will, endlessly adjusting and modifying themselves in conformity with the vast and otherwise enigmatic popular mind. Public participation in the stock market, then, was evidence of that most ardently desired ideological objective of all: popular consent to the deeds of American business. Thus it was the miracle of the Dow that provided the evangelists of the New Economy with one of their most potent economic arguments. Second only to the fall of Communism as 'proof' of the historical correctness of the corporate way, the ever-ascending Dow was what put the self-assured swagger in the New Economy consensus, what permitted Bill Clinton and his allies to declare that they alone could see the path of democratic righteousness, what put the seal of public approval on the politics of privatization, deregulation, deunionization, and the downgrading of the welfare state. Partisans of the new corporate order the world over pointed to the performance of the American stock markets the way politicians point to the 'mandate' given them by landslide electoral victories.[20]

A cursory examination of what shareholding actually means to the worker demonstrates that this is all pure poppycock.

. . . let us be clear about the stock market's actual contributions to economic democracy in the United States. However widely dispersed stock ownership may have become in recent years, the vast majority of shares are still held by the wealthy. It is this simple, incontestable fact of American life that, more than almost anything else, has permitted the massive skewing of wealth distribution in the last two decades. Stocks are the economic engine that has generally made the rich so very much richer than the rest of us, first through the bull market of the eighties and then through the bull market of the nineties. There is no controversy or secrecy about these facts: even an economist as partial to the New Economy as Lester Thurow acknowledges that America's widening inequality can be attributed directly to the rising stock market. A full 86 percent of the market's advances in the last four years of the bull market, he points out, went to the wealthiest 10 percent of the population. The majority of the population, not owning any stock, shared in the great money handout not at all.[21] The booming stock market of the nineties did not democratize wealth; it concentrated wealth.

Nor did stock prices reflect the growing prosperity of middle America. On the contrary, throughout the nineties stock prices consistently rallied on news that wages were lagging. The opposite was also true: reports of even marginal wage increases were sufficient throughout the duration of the People's Market to send the Dow into terrible fits and faints. And while millions of average white- and blue-collar workers saw their pension plans, 401(k)s, and IRAs appreciate nicely thanks to the deeds of the Dow, this hardly made up for the weak performance of wages. After all, workers can hardly be expected to own shares if they can't afford them. And even if everything went well – the market continued to perform so miraculously and all of us picked stocks that went up – the resulting gains would only ensure a few years of secure retirement in the distant future, not ease in the here-and-now.

As for the notion of representation through stockholding, it is important to remember that 'one dollar, one vote' is the definition of plutocracy, not democracy. While it is true that even the smallest of shareholders is entitled to attend companies' annual meetings and help themselves to the free radishes and nonalcoholic beer dispensed there, their votes are, in almost all cases, woefully insignificant in comparison to the massive clout wielded by institutional investors. In the case of mutual funds and pension plans, the instruments most frequently cited for their democratizing effects, individuals have even less of a voice. The voting is done for them – and by law, in the case of certain union pensions – by the manager of their plan or mutual fund.

Regardless of how we think about stocks or exactly how we kneel during our prayers to Wall Street, the nine years [as at 2005] of the last bull market only worsened what was already a spectacularly backward distribution of national wealth. Any claim that mass participation in the market has in some way brought economic democracy to the United States is false in a *prima facie* sense.[22]

The history of the 1970s and 1980s is, above all, a story of a smashing victory of the rich and powerful in their struggle to regain control after having had to share it with the people for two generations. The new policies did work though, in a way. Beggars returned to the streets of London and the number of millionaires rose spectacularly. The destruction of Keynesianism and its faint promise of a better world for ordinary people was complete.

Chapter 4

Honesty and value premises

In the previous chapter we saw a highly intelligent and learned economist, Friedrich von Hayek, express the following beliefs:
- Collective bargaining leads the worker to slavery.
- Full employment and low inflation are mutually incompatible.
- Free trade is beneficial to every nation and every person.
- A secure livelihood for all is incompatible with freedom.
- Laws guaranteeing effective competition can be made and enforced.
- Free markets guarantee the separation of political power from economic power.

None of these beliefs is backed by empirical evidence. It is therefore tempting to assume that von Hayek really had another – unexpressed – motivation, and used the specious claims above rather than say what he really stood for. With this *casus horribilis* as background, in this chapter I (Philip) will defend the proposition, first posed by Gunnar Myrdal, that the value of the social sciences depends to a large degree on the honesty with which scientists make clear what their *own* value premises are; that is, that they engage in neither self-deception nor misrepresentation.

Everyone who is either actively or passively involved in society makes valuations in regard to people, groups, occurrences and situations on and in the societal scene. Since the social scientist studies society, true objectivity – which would mean looking at the world from a vantage point outside of human life – is not possible, nor even imaginable. Self-examination of these valuations would then seem to be the minimum requirement that one should place on a social scientist. Not examining one's own biases and valuations is unfortunately more the norm than the exception in social scientific research. This is dishonest, since these valuations introduce biases that silently permeate and distort the structure and execution of the research and are therefore part and parcel of the conclusions reached. That is why honest social-scientific work demands that one state one's own valuations, so that another is aware of the biases and can arm himself or herself against them. The fact that this is seldom done severely reduces or nullifies the potential of social science for making a contribution to the solution of social problems.

The damage done to society by veiling the value premises behind work in social science is nowhere so serious as in economics, because economists are frequently in a position where they have great influence on political processes. And, although all leading economists declare, apparently with conviction, that the task of economics is to describe, and hopefully to understand, economic processes, but on no account to attempt to influence policy, in practice the run-of-the-mill economist does little else than just that. If then, as stated, hidden valuations lie behind this influence, civil society is not in a position to defend itself, especially since economists have achieved the status of experts despite their patent incapacity to predict economic developments. I would like to make it clear that this is not an academic or value-free issue. It concerns first and foremost the question of professional honesty, and is therefore central to this treatise. We return in later chapters to an examination of some important cases where it appears that a lack of honesty has led economists to outrageous conclusions.

An important contribution to honesty in the social sciences, included as an appendix to the classic study of the Negro 'problem' in the United States by Gunnar Myrdal,[1] was entitled 'Methods of Mitigating Biases in the Social Sciences'. Already in 1930 Myrdal's concern with the basic principle of economics, where concealed valuations were instrumental in shaping the theory, had resulted in his publishing a book on the political background of economic theory.[2] In this work, written soon after he gained his PhD, he showed how political valuations enter into the intellectual roots on which the various schools of economic thought have been based. He also, incidentally, dismantled the credibility of these assumptions by, on the one hand, showing them to be inconsistent or meaningless and, on the other, by showing them to bear practically no relation to the behaviour of human beings. It is reasonable to assume that his ruminations on the subject confronted him squarely with the dishonesty behind much highly respected economic theory, but he did not, as a very young academic, point this out clearly. Nonetheless, his acid comments on the lack of logic and even the meaninglessness of many accepted assumptions in various economic theories earned him the enduring dislike of many of his (elder) peers. It was in *An American Dilemma* that he squarely confronted the question of honesty for the first time. Many years later, in 1969, he published another book entirely devoted to the subject of objectivity in social research,[3] illustrating how this subject remained his lifelong preoccupation.

It is not my intention to go at length into the details of the failure of the various schools of economic thought to present a believable basis for understanding economic behaviour; there is a considerable body of literature showing that the assumptions on which economic theory is based cannot bear close examination. I will occasionally refer to the relevant publications, but not repeat all of the argumentation. The important aspects for our purpose are the ways in which hidden value premises are behind these failures.

But before discussing the way in which the hidden valuations wreak their havoc, let us return to the question of value premises themselves. I do this on the basis of Myrdal's own words. Although I admire his contribution to honest social science very highly, there is a certain point beyond which I can no longer go along with the way he proposes to choose value premises for a particular piece of research. This point of divergence is made explicit in the following.

Value premises

The following quotations cover the nucleus of Myrdal's arguments.

> . . . *biases in social science cannot be erased simply by 'keeping to the facts' and by refined methods of statistical treatment of the data.* Facts, and the handling of data, sometimes show themselves even more pervious to tendencies toward bias than does 'pure thought'. The chaos of possible data for research does not organize itself into systematic knowledge by mere observation. Hypotheses are necessary. We must raise questions before we can expect answers from the facts, and the questions must be 'significant'.

> . . . When, in an attempt to be factual, the statements of theory are reduced to a minimum, biases are left a freer leeway than if they were

more explicitly set forth and discussed. Neither can biases be avoided by the scientists' stopping short of drawing practical conclusions. *Science becomes no better protected against biases by the entirely negative device of refusing to arrange its result for practical and political utilization.* As we shall point out, there are, rather, reasons why the opposite is true. [4]

Our whole literature is permeated by value judgements, despite prefatory statements to the contrary. To the knowledge of the present writer, there is no piece of research on the Negro problem which does not contain valuations, explicit or implicit. Even when an author writing on, let us say, Negro education, politics, business, or labour attempts to give us only the data he has collected and the analysis he has made, he can rarely refrain from value judgements on them.

These practical judgements are usually relatively simple. They are not presented as inferences from explicit value premises plus the data, but rather, in the age-old fashion, as being evident from the nature of things: *actually as part of the objective data.* They are not marked off properly from theoretical knowledge of truth, but are most often introduced by loading part of the terminology with valuations, valuations which are kept vague and undefined. Sometimes the reader is told what is right or what is wrong, desirable or undesirable, only by implication.[5]

Biases in research are much deeper-seated than in the formulation of avowedly practical conclusions. They are not valuations *attached* to research but rather they *permeate* research. They are the unfortunate results of *concealed* valuations that insinuate themselves into research in all stages, from its planning to its final presentation. The valuations will, when driven underground, hinder observation and inference from becoming truly objective. This can be avoided only by making the valuations explicit. *There is no other device for excluding biases in social sciences than to face the valuations and to introduce them as explicitly stated, specific, and sufficiently concretized value premises.*[6]

There are only two means by which social scientists today avoid practical and political conclusions: (1) neglecting to state the value premises which, nevertheless, are implied in the conclusions reached;

(2) avoiding any rational and penetrating analysis of the practical problems in terms of social engineering (which would too visibly distract from the announced principles of being only factual). By the first restraint the doors are left wide open for hidden biases. The second inhibition prevents the social scientist from rendering to practical and political life the services of which he is capable."[7]

Up to this point I agree with Myrdal's arguments wholeheartedly. They seem to say that we can do nothing about our biases, but that by stating them explicitly we provide others with a tool to interpret our work in the light of their own experience. Unfortunately, the next step in his argument belies this impression, and it is from here on that I disagree with him. In describing his approach to *An American Dilemma*, Myrdal states:

The primary task in the present inquiry on the Negro problem has been to ascertain relevant facts and to establish the causal relations between facts. The viewpoints and, consequently, the principle of selection in regard to both direction and intensity of analysis, however, have been determined by certain value premises. In the practical sphere it has been our main task to ascertain how situations and trends, institutions and policies, have to be judged when a given set of value premises is applied.

The question of the selection of value premises remains to be settled. Values do not emerge automatically from the attempt to establish and collect the facts. Neither can we allow the individual investigator to choose his value premises arbitrarily. *The value premises should be selected by the criterion of relevance and significance to the culture under study*. Alternative sets of value premises would be most appropriate. If for reasons of practicability only one set of value premises is utilized, it is the more important that the reservation is always kept conscious: *that the practical conclusions – and, to an extent, the direction of research – have only hypothetical validity* and that the selection of another set of value premises might change both.[8]

I believe that it is impossible to do as Myrdal says, i.e. to *select* value premises in the way he prescribes. And if it were attempted, I think the results would be perniciously dishonest – dishonest because the researcher would be trying to be someone other than he or she actually is. Naturally, the value premises applied to a piece of research must be relevant and significant; it hardly seems necessary to stipulate that. But in my view one can not *choose* one's value premises. Whether through upbringing, schooling, reading or whatever, we all have relatively fixed valuations concerning the world about us, and, whether we like it or not, we carry them with us into our work in social science. Actually *choosing* alternative sets is essentially impossible unless one is an intellectual chameleon. I certainly cannot choose to examine economic reality through the glasses of Friedrich von Hayek (nor, incidentally, could Myrdal himself), however much I might want to, nor could I possibly describe the Second World War as seen through the eyes of an officer of the Waffen-SS. If I were to try to, my work would be even less honest than if I tried to hide my own, intrinsic, value premises. Further on in this chapter the reader will find these premises.

I believe that Myrdal spent his whole life searching for the will-o'-the-wisp of a true economic science that satisfied the 'rules' of the natural sciences. We see the heritage of the Enlightenment in his frequent use of words such as *scientific* and *objective*. In my view he would have been even more productive if he had dumped these words and accepted that *any* social science worthy of the name must have a strong normative element. In other words, in his world 'scientific' meant 'like physics', whereas for me the word 'scientific' means honest (in the sense of being critical of oneself and one's conclusions). That is why I can agree so thoroughly with most of his viewpoint on value premises, but not with his final conclusions.

This chapter concerns the value premises of economics, where make-believe has gone so far that most economists would even deny that economics *is* a social science at all, much less a moral science, as Adam Smith, John Maynard Keynes and Gunnar Myrdal, to name a few, believed it to be. More importantly – and that is what this chapter is mostly about – by pretending that social science can be carried out objectively without any values, the economist provides him- or herself with a 'back door' through which one's valuations can be smuggled into the results in an apparently innocent fashion. Myrdal's *The Political Element* catalogues the devices used in the different periods of the development of economic theory, beginning with the most naive, *natural law* (silently substituting *ought* for *is*), and going on to *utility* and later *marginal utility* to disguise the fact that there are real human needs, very many of which lie outside the domain of economic processes.

Looking at economics from the outside it is stupefying to see how much has been written about the measurability of utility and marginal utility – concepts that in most cases are far from rational and in any case are certainly not calculable.[9] Colouring the whole of economic theory, as well as the comments on it by Myrdal, is the heritage of the Enlightenment, which, by deifying reason, relegated to unmentionable obscurity all the values that make human life worth living.

The goal of this chapter is to uncover – or expose, if you like – the motivation behind this kind of thinking. I believe that there are two motives involved.

The first is the wish to 'look like' the hard sciences (physics and chemistry) and therefore to achieve 'respectability', since the world in general thinks that physics and chemistry are the 'highest' sciences. Allied to this motive there is also the haunting fear of saying something that people will consider to be irrational. Both this wish and this fear affect all scientific work, and are part and parcel of our heritage from the Enlightenment.

The second motive is the wish to espouse certain 'unmentionable' ideas without making clear what they are. Before considering this very loaded subject it is necessary to return to the discussion of value premises.

Naturally we all have many different kinds of value premises, so that for a given piece of research one must state those that are relevant to the case at hand. It would be wrong to suggest that exposing one's value premises is (ever) an easy task. It requires soul-searching, because we are all of us only partly aware of all of the baggage of beliefs that we carry with us. This baggage is usually called 'paradigms' when describing the *set of beliefs* that (practically speaking) all members of a given (sub)culture have in common. A paradigm is not experienced existentially as something you *believe to be true*, but as something that simply *is true*. Paradigms die hard, as the extraordinary case of Max Planck shows.[10] He would not have said that he *believed*, or that he *was of the opinion*, that light was continuous, because in his world, light *was* simply continuous.

But we also have, individually, our own set of values, some of which, at least, we have difficulty admitting are not truths but just our own personal opinions. Responsible social scientists know *themselves* and not just the subject matter of economy, sociology, psychology, or whatever discipline it may be, and make that self known to the audience. In this way the reader or listener is provided with a measuring stick by which to judge and place the scientist's work. I am of the opinion that all disciplines in the social sciences should encourage students to learn to know themselves, so that the social or moral sciences can become responsible again. One way of doing this would be to ask students, at intervals during the entire study, to describe their own values.

My (Philip's) value premises in writing this work

Lest I be accused of preaching purity to others while sinning myself, I summarize below what are, to the best of my introspective knowledge, my own value premises relevant to the subject of the way the world should be.

I believe that every human life has the same intrinsic value as mine. As a consequence of the need that I feel to have some say in the way I lead my life, democracy is for me the only acceptable way of organizing society. I am not opposed to competing if it means competition in promoting the common good. As far as basic rights are concerned, I hold that all must have the right to live in *dignity*; this means that I reject class distinction and racism.[11]

More specifically directed toward people's behaviour, I believe that to achieve an acceptable human community, society must shift its values away from *hardness*, *aggressiveness* and *competitiveness* toward *gentleness*, *compassion* and *sharing*; i.e. away from 'masculine' values toward 'feminine' values.

The value premises of mainstream economics

Since the main purpose of this treatise is to describe, from my point of view, the humanly negative world view of the mainstream economist, I cannot leave the subject without a comparison of my value premises with those of that economist. No two persons are the same, of course, and the totality of anyone's value premises is very complex. But the one value premise that seems to me to be common to all mainstream economists was described by the late Prince Claus of the Netherlands in a most succinct fashion.

It seems to me that if we look at the evolution of economic theory over the last two hundred years we can conclude, with tolerable exaggeration, that it has been basically concerned with the question of how those who are already rich, especially through their control of capital and land, can increase their wealth still further. Economists have given less attention to issues of distribution. Indeed, I believe that mainstream economics represents in many respects an orthodox consensus which can be shown to be deeply conservative. Such orthodoxy nearly always tells us we need more of the same that got us into the problem, to get us out of it again. It seldom tells us we need something new. Something different.[12]

I will now try to show that the theories and recommended policies of liberal economists support this interpretation. That does not prove that that is their goal. One may not impute goals to another, but only conclude on the basis of observable actions that these are, or are not, consistent with a given goal. The stated goal of liberal economics is 'efficient allocation'. It is not difficult to show that this leads irrevocably to the increase of riches of the wealthy, through the mechanism called the 'free market'.

I have used the word 'liberal' often, particularly in expounding the ideas of von Hayek. I use it in the European, not the North American, sense. A 'liberal' in the political sense should be taken in our text to mean a person whose goal is to grant the individual every freedom consistent with respect for the rights of others. In the economic sense, however, we define the 'liberal' as one who believes that economic activity should be competitive (specifically, not cooperative or collective). The State should do nothing except make sure that the conditions permitting competition are fulfilled. This does not mean a truly laissez-faire economic system, i.e. vanishing interference of the State in the economic affairs of its citizens. There can be considerable disagreement as to the extent to which the State must intervene to guarantee that competition takes place (and that it is 'fair', whatever that may mean).

The standpoints of the 'political liberal' and the 'economic liberal' are inconsistent (this inconsistency has, incidentally in our opinion, systematically undermined the coherence of the Liberal Party in England). The 'economic liberal' takes leave of the respect for the rights of others, characteristic of the 'political liberal', unless the 'other' belongs to the bourgeoisie. A 'good' economic system, in promulgating a 'level playing field', is blind to the gigantic difference in the bargaining power of rich and poor, of boss and worker; it therefore only bestows freedom on those with economic power, and thereby deprives those who do not have that power of their political rights. This is also relevant to the issue of class. Political liberalism holds that society should not be divided into classes. Rights are universal and are inalienable. But economic liberalism is built, silently, on class distinction. Accumulation of wealth depends on the existence of a labouring class whose wages can be kept low. That explains the opposition of economic liberals to workers' rights (e.g. collective bargaining, unemployment insurance, protection of the right to organise, etc.). It should be clear that this opposition is usually not expressed in so many words, but rather veiled in different wording, such as wording that expresses sympathy for the rights of workers. Examples are: 'collective bargaining deprives the individual worker of his/her right to get promoted and earn more by working hard', and 'unemployment insurance deprives the worker of the incentive to work'.

It should be noted that the economic liberal would vehemently deny that he or she supports laissez-faire, but would insist that, for example, the natural tendency of the market towards oligopoly and finally monopoly must be prevented by the regulative role of the government. One would have to search far, however, to find any opposition among liberal economists to the 'contraction' of markets by the rash of mergers and takeovers that are systematically destroying the last vestiges of fair competition in the modern Western economies. These are generally approved of by mainstream economists as increasing the competitiveness of a national economy. The approving stance taken by all leading liberal economists towards the smaller and smaller number of participants in the markets makes one doubt the sincerity of their rejection of laissez-faire.

Chapter 5

Imitation of the exact sciences: reductionism, mathematical models and Pareto

As already noted, it is not our intention to waste words on the shortcomings of economic theories. That has already been done more than adequately by a host of writers. The thrust of the present work is to argue that the inconsistencies and failings of economics came and come about because the primary purpose of the discipline is to serve the function of defending the status quo of wealth and power. Imitating the exact sciences kills two birds with one stone, as far as this is concerned. In the first place, if politicians believe that the statements of economists are *scientific*, these statements have a much greater chance of forming the basis of policy than if they were just the 'blather' of social scientists or moralists. But, more than that, it was (and still is to a great extent) generally accepted that the exact sciences are value-free, so statements of the practitioners are deemed to rise above the squabbles of everyday life and are clothed in the apparel of absolute truth. Two constructs adopted by economic thinking to this end are reductionism and mathematical models.

Reductionism

We begin with a discussion of the technique or practice of *reductionism*. This means abstracting from the total world around us a small part, and proceeding to study this part separately, explicitly assuming that there are no interactions with the rest of the world that could vitiate the validity of the results found.

Physics owes its reputation to its success in using this approach. One can study the atomic nucleus and arrive at valid conclusions, even though one ignores the world outside the nucleus, and, perhaps even more importantly, considers only a few of the myriad properties of the nucleus itself in explaining the particular experimental results in question. Reductionism is thus specifically and ideally suited to the study of (classes of) objects with limited interaction with other (classes of) objects, but, more importantly, studies where living – possibly irrational – beings, are excluded. Reductionism is frequently equated with *the scientific method* – a loosely defined way of working that, according to popular belief, all scientists follow. At best this is a caricature; nevertheless, the spectacular success of the hard sciences in describing simple, well-isolated phenomena in non-living nature made it (and its practitioners) the envy of all and the example to be followed in the study of anything.

Utility

It may have been partly this envy that inspired Jeremy Bentham to apply reductionism to human behaviour. He postulated that our total behaviour is explained by one moving force: the maximization of utility. One may surmise that this idea was inspired by simple non-relativistic (Newtonian) mechanics. The motion of heavenly bodies is, to a good approximation, entirely determined by only one thing – gravitation (and, of course, angular momentum; this is not a force but a property of Euclidean space). But to apply this same level of simplification to human behaviour requires a reductionist step of gigantic proportions. Gravitation can, after all, be precisely measured, and every physicist knows what it means. In contrast, it would be hard to find two persons who hold the same idea as to what utility *actually is*, let alone how it could be measured.

The point is that the reductionism involved in declaring utility to be the *only* motivating force of our behaviour served, and serves, a definite purpose as a bulwark against the introduction of ethical arguments in discussing the structure of society. It relieves the bourgeoisie from feelings of discomfort, since the bourgeoisie is so obviously successful in maximizing in their lives what they view as utility. Those who are unable to do this are simply lazy, or of weak character. Bentham went even further by declaring that the *good* and the *pleasurable* are synonymous – in one simple stroke eliminating the significance and relevance of several thousand years of serious thought on ethics, in particular the ethics of justice. The fact is, as any honest person will endorse, that what one finds pleasurable can, ethically or morally speaking, be not good at all, but rather very bad.

We feel that it is necessary to go further into the subject of 'pleasure' or 'happiness' before continuing. Many centuries of thinking, particularly by Hindu and Buddhist thinkers, point in a direction totally at odds with the hypothesis of Bentham that man is a "pleasure-seeking being". My (Philip's) particular favourite, which I try to let lead my life, is a little poem by the eighth-century sage Shantideva, about happiness.

> All the joy the world contains
> Has come through wishing happiness for others.
> All the misery the world contains
> Has come through wanting pleasure for oneself.

There are many more with similar messages, dating back more than 1,500 years. Although envy of the status of the exact sciences was most probably part of Bentham's motivation, it is safe to assume that building a defence of the status quo was the mainspring of his hypothesis. And it was certainly important for the almost universal, enthusiastic acceptance by economists (and of course by the wealthy of his time) of the idea that utility is the only motivating force in our behaviour. Neither Bentham nor Adam Smith before him seemed to have noticed that those who adhered in their actions most closely to the adage that seeking your own pleasure makes all of society richer, were just those who became immensely rich.

It is not, of course (following the Utilitarians' reductionist course, just for the sake of argument), the only possibility. After all, if Bentham sought only, as a physicist does, a single prime mover for human behaviour, he could have listened to the wisdom of the ages and equally well have postulated that fairness or compassion toward one's fellows is the unique driving force in our lives. This would have been a reductionistic exaggeration, just as the postulate of utility is. But there are untold numbers of people who are driven by the desire for fairness, who are guided in their lives by compassion for others; just as there are innumerable others who are driven by greed. But Bentham, as did Smith, chose to forget this kind of human being.

To postulate that *any simple* driving force can explain human behaviour may make one *look like* a physicist, but in this case appearances are quite deceiving. Bentham's reductionism served quite another social purpose, and for that purpose the particular choice of the driving force was essential. A discipline based on the premise that people are driven by compassion would have been an uneasy bedfellow with the rising spirit of capitalism in the eighteenth century. Bentham's choice was intuitive and easy. A ruling class that sent little children into the mines to work 12 hours a day and to be crippled by rickets could not be expected to look kindly at the hypothesis that compassion is an important stimulus in human behaviour – not to mention how the thoughts of Shantideva would have struck them.

Later in this book we shall examine the effect of economic thinking on the functioning of society in general. Our thesis is that if education were focused on teaching fairness and not competitiveness, the distribution of wealth in our world would look very different from how it actually does.

Ceteris paribus

Another kind of reductionism, which could be called 'logical reductionism', is commonly applied in economics to shut out the real world. In the real world of economics (and in human relations in general) everything is coupled to just about everything else, generally in complex irrational ways, which is the opposite of the situation in the exact sciences. Any measure taken by a government will bring about reactions that may go so far as to lead to a completely opposite result from what was intended, and any prediction of things to come can easily switch by 180° because of unexpected feedback. This being the empirical fact, if an economic calculation or reasoning points toward a certain result, it is customary when stating the prediction to append *ceteris paribus*, or 'other things being (and remaining) equal'. This is simply a rather cheap get-out clause. If things don't pan out the way one predicted they would, one simply says "Well, there was nothing wrong with the prediction, it's not my fault that *ceteris non paribus*." What one does, by making a prediction or judgement followed by *ceteris paribus*, is to say that one need attach no serious importance to what one has said. It reduces the value of what one says to silliness.

Mathematical models

Another enviable and status-raising characteristic of physics is its inextricable bond with mathematics. Toward the end of the nineteenth century Stanley Jevons took the step of mathematizing economics (this is discussed in more detail in Chapter 12). There were a few little problems, but economics, as an intellectual movement, rode roughshod over them. One of them, as the reader will remember from what we said earlier in this chapter about gravity, was that economists, in their headlong rush to make economics look like physics, brushed over the detail that it is of the essence that one can measure the fundamental quantities of a theory. To overcome that little problem, Jevons conceived of the hedonimeter, a device that could measure utility. Although no one had then, or has yet, the faintest idea of how it would work or what it would look like, the idea satisfied the profession. Having conceived the inconceivable, Jevons seemed to have satisfied his peers. It also had to be assumed that the maximization of utility proceeded along purely rational lines. Mathematics cannot be expected to describe irrational behaviour, so real, irrational, human behaviour was simply assumed not to exist. The fact that most human behaviour, especially when transactions are involved, is not rational, did not seem to form an obstacle to the adoption of Jevons' ideas. Unfortunately, social scientists and economists have tried to become respectable, in the sense of Isaac Newton, by peppering their scientific work with mathematical analysis. By ascribing rationality to people, one shuts oneself off from the possibility of discovering useful traits and behavioural quirks of real people that could help us understand the world – the economic world, in this case. Even more of a pity is that one also deprives oneself of the one tool that might help in deciphering human behaviour – one's own humanity. Jevons divorced economics from humanity and thus from the real world.

The Pareto optimum

Some of the ideas of economic theory, such as the hedonimeter or *ceteris paribus*, are just silly. But the ideas of Pareto are nasty. According to Pareto, a societal optimum exists when it is impossible to make anyone better off without making someone else worse off. This is a staggering statement, a barely camouflaged way of saying that the status quo is the best of all possible worlds. As in the case of the utility concept, this idea reduces the multitudinous factors determining our well-being to one thing – how much (of material things) we possess. Such an idea goes against any broad view of human value, but one must be naive indeed not to notice that this definition is quite suitable for reassuring those loaded with possessions that it would be bad for society, *as a whole*, if they were to have less. It is interesting to note that when marginal utility became an important part of economic theory, because no economic equilibrium could be conceived unless utility tapered off somehow with increasing possessions, the Pareto optimum came, or should have come, under stress. The obvious consequence of the idea of marginal utility is that if utility tapers off when possessions increase, then the total utility of a community will increase if wealth is taken away from the rich and given to the poor. This is an unthinkable hypothesis in economic theory. The intellectual antics that followed were quite humorous, as one can experience by reading about the debate between Harrod and Robbins.[1] As a community, economists solved the problem (which in essence raised a doubt about the possibility of economics as a serious intellectual pursuit) by keeping to the idea of marginal utility when needed for equilibrium, but forgetting about it when discussing the way society should be, for instance via the Pareto optimum.

There have been many erudite discussions concerning 'the way society should be'. One important contributor was Pigou, whose definition of welfare was tainted with egalitarianism and therefore quite incompatible with a Pareto optimum. The fact that mainstream economics greeted Pareto's ideas with enthusiasm and Pigou's with silence (or worse) is one more brick in the foundation of our original premise that the function of economics in society is to support an inequitable status quo.

Mathematics was simply built into the laws that describe the behaviour of the atomic nucleus. You didn't have to impose it on the nucleus. You simply couldn't live without it. In sociology, and certainly in economics, mathematics is imposed on human behaviour. This book is a study of economics, which is extremely relevant to all that lives. We say "all that lives", because human ideas affect animals and plants – think of the destruction of biodiversity and the poisoning of the ecosphere caused by the human (actually inhuman) doctrine of endless economic growth. This imitation of the exact sciences by economics is an epistemological aberration, just exactly because the preoccupation of the social sciences with mathematics hides the indescribable, intensely beautiful, complexity of life: a complexity that defies any meaningful mathematical analysis. But worse, as argued earlier, this imitation deprives the practitioner of the one tool – humanity – that could lead to real understanding.

Chapter 6

Economic growth

Growth as a shibboleth

The beliefs of different people are tremendously diverse, and more often than not mutually contradictory. There is one belief, or conviction, however, that almost everyone in today's world agrees on: economic growth is good, even necessary. Conventional wisdom holds that economic growth will bring riches and happiness to all (or at least to all who count), and in the daily news it is universally assumed, as an eternal truth, that high growth is good and low growth, not to mention contraction, is bad. Even now, in the post-modern period when dreams of endless progress have gone a bit stale, economic growth remains the beckoning buoy toward which all humankind must sail. Even many ecological economists have difficulty accepting that continued growth will make their goal of humankind being at peace with the biosphere unattainable.

Economic growth brings a continuously rising level of material well-being to the well-to-do. But there are a great many who do not profit materially from economic growth. In fact, after several centuries of economic growth the majority of the world's population still has less in the way of housing, food and infrastructure than the rock-bottom minimum needed to live a secure and dignified life. Economic growth is not improving their lot. Not all of those so deprived live in the poor countries; there are many in the rich countries who live in grinding, futureless poverty. Apart from its deleterious effects on the biosphere, the tragedy of economic growth is that it is producing, in the world of today, growing mountains of goods and services for a minority of the world's population, while simultaneously denying to the impoverished even a bare minimum of the wherewithal for a decent life. It is all the more poignant that when the crunch comes, as shown by the crisis that began in October

2008, it will be the poorest and the middle class, those who have in no way profited from the present economic growth, who will pay the highest price.

What economic growth is doing

Although only a minority of the world's population profits substantially from economic growth, it is having disastrous effects on a world-wide scale. In short, economic growth:

- is poisoning the biosphere at an increasing rate with pollutants, some of which are not only extremely persistent but threaten fundamental life processes.

- is exhausting the immense stocks of raw materials with which nature has endowed the inhabitants of the Earth, to the point that some stocks, in particular stocks of energy sources, will be exhausted within the lifetime of many – perhaps most – of those now living. The threat of exhaustion is leading to wars for control of the remaining stocks, wars in which thousands of innocent people have already died. Unless the growth fetish is resolutely renounced, more wars will be fought for access to dwindling resources in the coming decades, causing terrible human suffering and reshaping the geopolitical landscape of the globe with unforeseeable consequences.

- creates a steadily increasing stream of wealth of which by far the largest part goes to the already rich and powerful. Some small part of the stream trickles down to the poor. But inherently, at least in a (free) market economy, economic growth increases the proportion of the stream that goes to the already rich. In recent decades, due to a number of consequences of the application of neoliberal economic practice, even the 'trickle-down' has dried up, leaving the poor with even less means to live on and less hope for the future than in the past, while the number of rich, very rich, and ultra-rich continues to increase rapidly.

- combined with population growth, is destroying the habitat of the species that share the biosphere with us, causing an increasing rate of extinction that will, in time, lead to the impoverishment of all life.

What this all comes down to is that economic growth has thwarted and will, in increasing measure, continue to thwart any and every effort to bring about a world in which all can live in peace and security. Although lip-service is paid to the necessity for measures directed toward bringing about such a world, the course followed by all political leaders gives the highest priority to growth. This is adamantly adhered to, even though the very short period (relative to the total history of humankind) of accelerated economic growth made possible by the combustion of fossil fuels is drawing rapidly to a close. In order to avoid the foreseeable human catastrophes that an abrupt end to this period would cause, it is absolutely necessary to immediately put policies in place to bring about first a levelling off, and then the beginning of a slow contraction in the economy. Yet there is no sign that any such change in policy is in the offing, while the essence of the consequences just described is that economic growth and population growth are responsible for the ongoing degradation of the life-supporting capacity of the world – the only world we have; the world where our great-grandchildren will have to live.

The voices for growth

But are our political leaders really the ones to blame? Are they deliberately leading the world to disaster? Political leaders have to decide on policy in the midst of a cacophony of opposing interests and opinions. And since it is economists who have been adorned with the mantle of wisdom in our society, it is not surprising that politicians listen first and foremost to the leading economists in deciding policy. Arguments brought in by voices of sanity are not listened to. Arguing with mainstream economists is difficult because the belief in infinite growth has religious characteristics. In preaching the theology of growth, the economist contends that there are economic 'laws' that guarantee that economic growth can continue forever without exhausting our resources, while concomitantly increasing welfare and bringing about a progressively cleaner environment. (At the end of this chapter it is shown that these 'laws' have no empirical basis. It is doubtful, however, if this will influence mainstream economists to think differently.) This point of view is exemplified by the words of the late Julian Simon, a respected economist, written in 1995.

> Technology exists now to produce in virtually inexhaustible quantities just about all the products made by nature – foodstuffs, oil, even pearls and diamonds – and make them cheaper in most cases than the cost of gathering them in their natural state. . . . We have in our hands now – actually, in our libraries – the technology to feed, clothe, and supply energy to an ever-growing population for the next 7 billion years.[1]

Earlier, Simon had presented a logically impeccable proof that our supply of copper can never be exhausted.

> The length of a one-inch line is finite in the sense that it is bounded at both ends. But the line within the endpoints contains an infinite number of points; these points cannot be counted, *because* they have no defined size. Therefore the number of points in that one-inch segment is not finite. *Similarly*, the quantity of copper that will ever be available to us is not finite, *because* there is no method (even in principle) of making an appropriate count of it.[2] [Our italics]

Simon's is only one of many similar voices.[3] As the signs become clearer and clearer that endless economic growth is not only mathematically ridiculous but is leading the world at an accelerated pace toward disaster, the voices of those who proclaim that it is the ultimate cure for all our problems become louder and louder. If one speaks loudly enough, one can no longer hear the ticking of the clock. One must ask, though, whether politicians have much choice. Those who advise caution in our treatment of the world we live in are, in fact, speaking for future generations, and future generations have neither political clout nor financial support. Those pushing for economic growth have both, in large measure. The choice of who to listen to is quickly made.

Bjørn Lomborg, who has published on game theory and computer simulations, is a good example of the latter lobby. He believes that if economic growth could be made high enough (over 10 per cent), most of our problems would be solved.[4] Not surprisingly, he has solid financial support from the business world for his activities, in no small measure because he is dead set against abiding by the terms of the Kyoto Protocol. In May 2004 he was able to raise sufficient financial support (more than $800,000) to convene a meeting in Copenhagen, under the title 'Copenhagen Consensus' of an impressive panel of "economic experts, comprising eight of the world's most distinguished economists", three of whom were Nobel Laureates.

These panellists judged the priority that should be given to the solution of a number of 'challenges' facing humankind. These were posed by a group of experts, each of whom presented a 'Challenges Paper'. The conclusions of the panel were based purely on monetary cost–benefit analysis; no societal or ethical factors were considered. Curing disease, for example, was rated according to the monetary benefits and costs associated with it. Two projects that rated *Very Good* were the control of HIV/AIDS (priority 1) and malaria (priority 4). Providing micro-nutrients (not food) to the starving was also rated *Very Good* (priority 2). The Kyoto Protocol was almost at the bottom of the list, rated *Bad* (priority 16).

These remarkable priorities become even more interesting when one reviews the list of the names of the panellists and the 'challengers'. They were drawn from that segment of economic thought with an unqualified belief in economic growth. Not one has either medical or nutritional science qualifications, nor were there any with (professional) knowledge of climate change. Lomborg claims that priorities of different policy options should be set by economists whose professional knowledge reaches no further than the calculated financial consequences of the options.[5] This is indeed sad, since the problem, a problem about life, goes much beyond mere finance.

It should be mentioned that there are quite a few other very distinguished economists not chosen by Lomborg, including Nobel Prize winners, who accord priority to the Kyoto Protocol. Naturally everyone has their right to an opinion, but to use the word 'consensus' for the opinion of Lomborg's panel is like claiming the status of consensus for the opinion of a panel of Roman Catholic cardinals who say that the Pope is infallible.

The voices acclaiming the benefits of continuing economic growth are many, but the relatively few dissenting voices are seldom heard. In the following we present arguments to help make the latter voices more audible.

Two incompatible systems

One reason why the economy is addicted to growth was pinpointed by the remarkable maverick thinker, M. King Hubbert, as follows.

> The world's present industrial civilization is handicapped by the coexistence of two universal, overlapping, and incompatible intellectual systems: the accumulated knowledge of the last four centuries of the properties and interrelationships of matter and energy; and the associated monetary culture which has evolved from folkways of pre-historic origin.
>
> The first of these two systems has been responsible for the spectacular rise, principally during the last two centuries, of the present industrial system and is essential for its continuance. The second, an inheritance from the pre-scientific past, operates by rules of its own, having little in common with those of the matter–energy system. Nevertheless, the monetary system, by means of a loose coupling, exercises a general control over the matter–energy system upon which it is superimposed.
>
> Despite their inherent incompatibilities, these two systems during the last two centuries have had one fundamental characteristic in common, namely exponential growth, which has made a reasonably stable coexistence possible. But, for various reasons, it is impossible for the matter–energy system to sustain exponential growth for more than a few tens of doublings, and this phase is by now almost over. The monetary system has no such constraints, and, according to one of its most fundamental rules, it must continue to grow by compound interest.[6]

Looked at in this way, growth is forced on us, willy-nilly, by the custom of measuring wealth in terms of money. This brings about the appearance of spontaneous increase of wealth by compound interest, a sort of abiogenesis impossible with real wealth. It is clear that without an external source of energy, in this case fossil fuels, the growth syndrome would not have become so important.

The monetary system – in short, the idea that all wealth, all value, can be expressed in terms of so much money – is embedded in our whole culture. It is embedded so deeply that when a group of (mostly) exact scientists was called upon by the United Nations Development Programs (UNDP), The United Nations Department of Economic and Social Affairs (UNDESA), and the World Energy Council (WEC) to make an assessment of the world's energy use and availability, the assessment (WEA) was carried out entirely in monetary units, which are quite meaningless in the assessment of energy use and energy carriers. A meaningful assessment can only be made in energy units (joules). We return to the question of assessment of energy sources shortly.

Compound interest and wealth

Other writers[7] have spelled out in detail the unavoidable negative consequences for human well-being and social stability of, and the religious nature of the belief in, growth as the great panacea. But there seems to be little awareness that the monetary intellectual system is an integral part of modern society's world view, and how it forces the economy to grow (or else wither). Frederick Soddy, a Nobel-Prize-winning natural scientist who understood economy better than most economists, exposed the error in reasoning that has led practically everyone to accept the widespread misconception that compound interest *creates* wealth. It does not create wealth at all, but rather debt. It diverts a continually increasing part of the stream of wealth created by the productive sector of the population and transfers it to the creditors, frequently leaving the wealth-producer holding the (empty) bag.

But first, what is wealth? A reasonable definition of wealth is that proposed by Soddy, and recently summarized by Herman Daly.

> For Soddy the basic economic question was 'How does man live?' and the answer was 'By sunshine'. The rules that man must obey in living on sunshine, whether current or palaeozoic, are the first and second laws of thermodynamics. This in a nutshell is 'the bearing of physical science upon state stewardship'.[8] Wealth is for Soddy 'the humanly useful forms of matter and energy'.[9] Wealth has both a physical dimension, matter–energy subject to the laws of inanimate mechanism, and a teleological dimension of usefulness, subject to the purposes imposed by mind and will. Soddy's concept of wealth reflects his fundamental dualism and his belief that the middle world of life

and wealth is concerned with the interaction of the two end worlds of physics and mind in their commonest everyday aspects. That Soddy concentrated on the physical dimension in order to repair the consequences of its past neglect should not be allowed to lead one to suppose that he proposed a monistic physical theory of wealth.[10]

What should be clear from this exposition is that debts are not wealth. Wealth has an irreducible physical dimension and debt is a purely mathematical, or imaginary quantity. An essential property of wealth is that it is a stream, practically all of which is produced on a daily basis and expended within a short time. Some forms of wealth have a certain permanency, though. It is not necessary to try to evaluate how much wealth can actually be stored, or for how long, in order to get an overall picture. Even that part of wealth that can be stored is slowly reduced to zero by depreciation and rot. What is important is that wealth is real and debt is not. As Daly puts it, "the positive physical quantity, two pigs, represent wealth and can be seen and touched. But *minus* two pigs, debt, is an imaginary magnitude with no physical dimension."[11] This is far from an unimportant difference, as Soddy explains.

> Debts are subject to the laws of mathematics rather than physics. Unlike wealth, which is subject to the laws of thermodynamics, debts do not rot with old age and are not consumed in the process of living. On the contrary, they grow at so much per cent per annum, by the well-known mathematical laws of simple and compound interest. . . . The process of compound interest is physically impossible, though the process of compound decrement is physically common enough. Because the former leads with passage of time ever more and more rapidly to infinity, which, like minus one, is not a physical but a mathematical quantity, whereas the latter leads always more slowly towards zero . . . the lower limit of physical quantities.[12]

The source, or raw material, from which wealth is produced, was, during much the longest part of humankind's history, only sunlight acting upon living and dead matter, organized through human effort. Hydrocarbons laid aside by life processes, long before humans came into being, have recently been added to the source of wealth production. These are now, since a few hundred years ago, in the process of being used (up), thereby making a larger stream of wealth *temporarily* possible. These hydrocarbons are exceedingly important, as is clear from the reasoning of Hubbert, quoted on page 74, for the functioning of our present industrial society. Without them the whole concept of compound interest would not have become as important as it is.

The following quotation from Daly, drawing on publications of Soddy, again concurs with Hubbert's thesis that real wealth can grow for a time only, but debt (not being real) can grow to infinity.

> Although debt can follow the law of compound interest, the real energy revenue from future sunshine, the real future income against which the debt is a lien, cannot grow at compound interest for long. When converted into debt, however, real wealth 'discards its corruptible body to take on an incorruptible'.[13] In so doing, it appears 'to afford a means of dodging Nature',[14] of evading the second law of thermodynamics, the law of random, ravage, rust, and rot. The idea that people can live off the interest of their mutual indebtedness is just another perpetual motion scheme – a vulgar delusion[15] on a grand scale. . . . Debt grows at compound interest and as a purely mathematical quantity encounters no limits to slow it down. Wealth grows for a while at compound interest, but, having a physical dimension, its growth sooner or later encounters limits. Debt can endure forever; wealth cannot, because its physical dimension is subject to the destructive force of entropy. Since wealth cannot continually grow as fast as debt, the one-to-one relation between the two will at some point be broken – i.e. there must be some repudiation or cancellation of debt.[16]

Real debts and the energy costs of energy

Although, as explained above, monetary debts are not real, real debts can exist. Knowing the dollar cost of extracting an energy carrier from the crust of the Earth can be useful for a businessman looking for profit, but the real cost can be given only in matter–energy units; in this case the total energy cost of (1) extraction, purification and removal from the biosphere of polluting products of the carrier and of the waste produced by the purification and extraction, and (2) the energy used in construction and later decommissioning of the plant that converts the energy carrier into useful energy, plus operating costs (expressed in energy units). The energy value of the carrier is the total useful energy delivered minus the sum of these costs.

To take an example: consider that we haven't the faintest idea how much *net* energy humankind has extracted from the fossil fuels burned in the last two centuries. This is because the energy cost of removing the pollutants from the biosphere, particularly the CO_2 (to at least a level that would guarantee that life on Earth, as we now know it, will not be threatened), is completely unknown, simply because this removal has not even been seriously contemplated. Burning fossil fuels without considering this cost indicates an *après nous le déluge* attitude – an attitude that we in the rich countries are all guilty of, to a greater or lesser degree. If the production of CO_2 and other pollutants were to be drastically reduced, the interlocking, symbiotic living systems of the biosphere would finally 'pay' the debt for humankind in the course of centuries. If, on the contrary, the CO_2 emissions stay the same as today or increase further, they will finally wreak havoc on all that lives, overpowering the resilience of the life-supporting capacity of the biosphere.

Or consider the disposal of the radioactive pollution left behind by the fission reaction in nuclear (power and weapons-materials) reactors. These pollutants constitute a real debt that humankind will have to pay. The biosphere has no defence against radioactivity, although, through radioactive decay, nature will eventually pay the debts herself, but only in a time frame of hundreds of thousands of years. That such a time frame is of no relevance for humankind should give pause for thought.

In this and most other cases of physical debt it is only meaningful to express this debt in energy units (joules), which are not only real, but conserved. The egregious financial custom of discounting the (monetary) value of resources is therefore not applicable to energy sources, although it is erroneously used in financial calculations and policy. In the monetary system where value is expressed in non-physical terms (money), a debt that cannot be paid can be wiped off the ledger as a 'bad debt': it is not a conserved quantity. But in the real world of matter and energy, debts are anything but arbitrary, and will be paid, if not in energy and matter then in the suffering of the living systems of the biosphere.

That such real energy debts are piling up, unpaid, means that we are living in a fool's paradise. Public awareness of this is systematically discouraged by business organizations only interested in the quarterly bottom line, and their spiritual confrères, the mainstream economists.

Not all debts that humankind has built up through bad housekeeping can be expressed in energy terms. Worth mentioning are the persistent organochlorides, poisonous to all life, that have been produced by the chemical industry and are present in easily measurable quantities in mothers' milk all over the globe. Other units would have to be used to express this debt, but as far as we know we have no means of repaying it, while the production continues, in most cases unabated.

Compound interest, peak oil and the end of growth

What compound interest does for the creditor is quite different from what it does to the debtor. If a debt was just a debt until paid back, with or without a certain percentage added to it, then it would not bring about a long-term increase in the diversion of the wealth stream from the debtor to the creditor. But with compound interest in the game a steadily increasing stream of wealth is diverted from the debtor to the creditor, long after the original diversion, presumably for useful purposes, has ceased.

When money is borrowed by wealth producers, a steadily growing fraction of the wealth created by their productive work is thereafter diverted to the creditor from the total stream of produced wealth. In order for the total system to maintain itself without progressively impoverishing the productive sector there must be a steadily increasing stream of wealth produced. The essence of Hubbert's argument is that as long as there is a continuously growing use of fossil fuels, added to the constant input from sunlight, the two systems, matter and energy on the one hand, and money on the other, can coexist. As long as this condition persists, it appears, superficially, that it is 'natural' that the use of energy and matter from the Earth's crust grows continuously.

It is, in fact, quite unnatural; and in the long period before the steadily growing use of fossil fuels made it possible, it didn't happen – and people did not

think that growth was a normal thing. Over the course of millennia, improvements in agriculture progressively raised the yield of solar energy and made
larger populations viable, but these were gradual changes that did not seem
to change people's way of thinking. The exceptionally abrupt but, above all,
quantitatively enormous increase brought about by the use of fossil fuels did,
however, so that today most people believe that growth is normal and can
continue indefinitely. When the time comes that the growth in the use of
fossil fuels ceases, the coexistence of the two systems will become impossible, and the extremely painful adjustment to non-growth will take place.

Note that this adjustment will occur before fossil fuels are *exhausted*. The
turning point – i.e. the point at which the matter–energy system can no
longer keep up with the monetary system and the financial structure of society will have to be shored up to prevent total collapse, with at present unim-
aginable measures – occurs much earlier, in fact, not too long after the *growth*
of fossil fuel use stops.[17] It is frightening to picture what will happen when the
vast financial structures, on which everything we own and do floats, are no

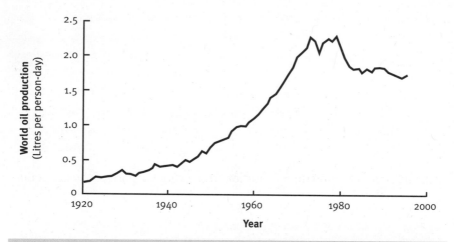

Figure 1. World daily production of petroleum per capita has been steadily dropping
since the 1970s, when it was roughly 2 litres per person-day. Currently, US consumption is about 4 litres per person-day. As petroleum production struggles to keep up
with growing demand, and as world population continues to grow, it is unlikely that
world per capita production can ever again rise to the levels reached in the 1970s.

longer viable. During a full half-century, from 1950 to 2000, there was yearly more petroleum found than was pumped out of the wells. But for several years now, there is more being pumped up than is being found. Even more ominous is the fact that world oil production per capita reached a maximum 30 years ago and has since gone steadily downward. This is shown in Figure 1, taken from a publication by Albert Bartlett.[18]

There will be many crises when oil begins to get scarce. The following is only one, though perhaps the most ghastly. The highly productive grains developed in the so-called 'Green Revolution', which both led to and made possible the greatest explosion of population in humankind's history, can be grown thanks only to large inputs of artificial fertilizers and pesticides. These are industrial products, the manufacture of which depends directly on the readily available energy in oil. This translates into several billions of people being alive at this moment because of the *temporary* extra energy input (beyond that of sunlight) of petroleum. When this is depleted there will be no way to feed the entire population of the Earth, and mass starvation will be inevitable. Optimists see the present decrease of the growth in oil discovery and production as an aberration, and assume that the tempo of discovery will soon rise again. This may happen, but even so such a rise will certainly not last more than another decade. Continuous growth within a physically finite system is then certain to stop. The question is in what way.

The inversion of the roles of production and wants

Besides the coexistence of the two inherently incompatible systems discussed above, which are leading us like a Pied Piper into the cul-de-sac of endless growth, there is another reason, different from but not unrelated to the first, for the addiction to growth: a distortion in the very purpose of the economic system. We refer here to the inversion of the roles of production and wants. Traditionally, goods and services are produced to satisfy needs (or at least wants). So, in the minds of most people, the satisfaction of wants is the driving force in the economic system. And for much the longest part of humankind's history this was a correct description of what production was for. But in the rich countries of the globe this relationship between production and wants has now been inverted.

Production for the sake of production, not the satisfaction of wants, is today the primary goal of the economy, and in order to keep it rolling, new wants must continually be created. Advertising is the instrument for this creation, and will be discussed later. The inversion did not take place overnight, but has been slowly developing for more than a century. In the last decades of the twentieth century, the process accelerated and one can now say that it has been completed. The mouths of economists, but also of all manner of other pundits, are today full of the necessity to increase productivity, so as to increase production, in a society drowning in things that are not needed and could not be sold were it not for the ever-present influence of advertising. The spectre of financial collapse if production does not keep increasing is called up to still the few sane voices who protest.

Since this inversion provides an automatic justification of endless economic growth, mainstream economists have necessarily found the means to incorporate it into theory without actually calling it by name. John K. Galbraith has the following to say.

> Production cannot be an incidental to the mitigation of inequality or the provision of jobs. It must have a *raison d'être* of its own. At this point, economists and economic theory have entered the game. So, more marginally, does the competitive prestige that goes with expanding national product. The result has been an elaborate and ingenious defence of the importance of production as such. It is a defence which makes the urgency of production largely independent of the volume of production. In this way, economic theory has managed to transfer the sense of urgency in meeting consumer need that once was felt in a world where more production meant more food for the hungry, more clothing for the cold, and more houses for the homeless to a world where increased output satisfies the craving for more elegant automobiles, more exotic food, more erotic clothing, more elaborate entertainment – indeed, for the entire modern range of sensuous, edifying and lethal desires.

Although the economic theory which defends these desires and hence the production that supplies them has an impeccable (and to an astonishing degree even unchallenged) position in the conventional wisdom, it is illogical and meretricious and, in degree, even dangerous.[19]

These facts form together the underlying mechanism that leads the affluent societies of the globe to fetishize the growth that is causing environmental destruction so serious that it could quite possibly threaten the future of life. Can they be combatted?

John Maynard Keynes, Thorstein Veblen and emulation

How could our society be organized, or be motivated, to appreciate the value of that simple word, 'enough'? Help in answering this question can be found in the vision of one who anticipated the present surplus productive capacity and predicted (quite wrongly, as it turns out) what it would lead to. Eighty years ago Keynes gave his vision of the future when what he called *the economic problem* had been solved. These thoughts were expressed in a chapter entitled 'Economic possibilities for our grandchildren' (from a speech given in 1930) of *Essays in Persuasion*, published in 1931.

> Let us, for the sake of argument, suppose that a hundred years hence we are all of us, on the average, eight times better off in the economic sense than we are to-day. Assuredly there need be nothing here to surprise us.

> . . . I draw the conclusion that, assuming no important wars and no important increase in population, the *economic problem* may be solved, or be at least within sight of solution, within a hundred years. This means that the economic problem is not – if we look into the future – *the permanent problem of the human race.*

> Why, you may ask, is this so startling? It is startling because if – instead of looking into the future, we look into the past – we find that the economic problem, the struggle for subsistence, always has been hitherto the primary, most pressing problem of the human race . . . Thus we have been expressly evolved by nature – with all our

impulses and deepest instincts – for the purpose of solving the economic problem. If the economic problem is solved, mankind will be deprived of its traditional purpose.

Will this be a benefit? If one believes at all in the real values of life, the prospect at least opens up the possibility of benefit. Yet I think with dread of the readjustment of the habits and instincts of the ordinary man, bred into him for countless generations, which he may be asked to discard within a few decades. . . . For many ages to come the old Adam will be so strong in us that everybody will need to do *some* work if he is to be contented. . . . Three-hour shifts or a fifteen-hour week may put off the problem for a great while.

There are changes in other spheres too which we must expect to come. When the accumulation of wealth is no longer of high social importance, there will be great changes in the code of morals. We shall be able . . . to assess the money-motive at its true value. The love of money as a possession – as distinguished from the love of money as a means to the enjoyments and realities of life – will be recognised for what it is, a somewhat disgusting morbidity, one of those semi-criminal, semi-pathological propensities which one hands over with a shudder to the specialists in mental disease. All kinds of social customs and economic practices, affecting the distribution of wealth and of economic rewards and penalties, which we now maintain at all costs, however distasteful and unjust they may be in themselves, because they are tremendously useful in promoting the accumulation of capital, we shall then be free, at last, to discard.[20]

But it is exactly here that Keynes missed the point. However gigantic the scale of production has become, and even though the accumulation of capital has risen beyond the limits of any conceivable usefulness, the accumulation of wealth remains, and will remain, of overriding social importance. This was explained by Thorstein Veblen, on the basis of observation of the world about him and a thorough study of existing anthropological evidence, as the consequence of the drive toward emulation.

The end of acquisition and accumulation is conventionally held to be the consumption of the goods accumulated – whether it is consumption directly by the owner of the goods or by the household attached to him and for this purpose identified with him in theory. This is at least felt to be the economically legitimate end of acquisition, which alone it is incumbent on the theory to take account of. Such consumption may of course be conceived to serve the consumer's physical wants – his physical comfort – or his so-called higher wants – spiritual, æsthetic, intellectual, or what not; the latter class of wants being served indirectly by an expenditure of goods, after the fashion familiar to all economic readers.

But it is only when taken in a sense far removed from its naive meaning that consumption of goods can be said to afford the incentive from which accumulation invariably proceeds. The motive that lies at the root of ownership is emulation; and the same motive of emulation continues active in the further development of the institution to which it has given rise and in the development of all those features of the social structure which this institution of ownership touches. The possession of wealth confers honor; it is an invidious distinction. Nothing equally cogent can be said for the consumption of goods, nor for any other conceivable incentive to acquisition, and especially not for any incentive to the accumulation of wealth.[21]

The drive to emulate others, in particular one's peers, in the acquisition of property, as observed by Veblen, is synonymous with competitiveness – a polite word for greed. In Chapter 3 we saw that competitiveness was the essential hallmark of the 'good society' as envisioned by von Hayek.

In a way, Keynes's naivety is touching. That such a brilliant man did not, could not, see the real reason behind the 'love of money' is because he was schooled in economic theory: a theory that has never really seriously mulled over, but has rather blindly accepted, Bentham's postulate of utility. Later on, in order to allow the construction of mathematical models of economic equilibrium (an unobserved phenomenon that therefore actually needs no explanation), the concept of marginal utility gained acceptance. It is presumed in theory that as a person becomes rich the desire to get richer slowly peters out.

This is quite at loggerheads with the actual motivation behind the accumulation of wealth, as explained by Veblen. Each marginal increment of income can even, in exceptionally predatory societies, such as the present society has become in the last decades under the influence of neoliberalism, be felt to have an *in*creasing utility. The existence of growing numbers of billionaires, and the respect that is accorded them, testifies to this.

On the other hand, Keynes's prediction of a tremendous increase in the material well-being of people in the rich countries[22] is certainly not far off the mark. And incidentally, what an insight his lovely vision of the future gives into the thought, and the limitations in the thought, of one of the handful of highly influential economists of the twentieth century! But that is not the subject of this book and we will not go into it any further than to note that this one quotation of Keynes makes it clear why others, von Hayek in particular, disliked Keynes's ideas so intensely.

Advertising

In order that the services and products of an endlessly increasing production can be sold, a demand for them must be created. The task of cranking up wants belongs in the realm of advertising. In the advertising to which we are exposed, the theme of emulation plays an important, though usually disguised, role. To get the 'emulation value' across, highly trained psychologists are recruited who avail themselves of the most advanced techniques of psychological manipulation. To do what? To create demand where there would otherwise be none.

One who believes that advertising has the goal of presenting the consumer with objective facts has indeed lost contact with reality. Almost the entire advertising industry is occupied with the task of making people want things that they do not need. It can superficially be described as an unproductive fringe to our economic system. Our thesis is that it is much more than this; it is the instrument by which growth is continuously stimulated, and thereby the attitude of 'always more' is instilled in the public mind. It is advertising that has made it possible to invert the role of production and wants.

In calculating their Index of Sustainable Economic Welfare (ISEW) for the United States, Daly and Cobb[23] do subtract the cost of national advertising from welfare, although local advertising is not taken into account. They argue that local advertising may have value to the consumer, but, in their words, "By contrast, national advertising (especially on television and in magazines) tends to be aiming at creating demand for products and brand-name loyalty through the use of images that have little to do with the actual product."

While we have no quarrel with the treatment presented by Daly and Cobb, we think that the significance of advertising is not treated seriously enough by simply assigning to it a negative contribution to sustainable human welfare. Its most important effect is to degrade human values. Its effect is much more penetrating than just to induce people to buy things that they do not need. It affects almost every facet of people's lives. Particularly damaging to human value in the advertisements for durable goods, as mentioned already, is the veiled approbation of emulative behaviour, implying the identity of one's value with one's possessions.

One could go on at length about the morally egregious influence of advertising on the body politic, but we leave it here with one more remark: by continually accentuating the fiction that having things gives meaning to life, and, even further, by implying that without the possession of a superabundance of material things life loses its meaning, advertising demeans life itself.

Since it is the motor of economic growth, it is quite remarkable that advertising is not even mentioned in standard economic texts. This is easily explained. Since economic theory postulates that wants are intrinsic to the consumer, and invariant as well, it is by definition theoretically of no importance whatsoever whether advertising exists or not. Yet one does not have to be very clever to realize that modern economic activity would collapse without it.

The role of economists

The only logical conclusion at this point is that great haste must be made to educate the public that growth must stop, and stop soon enough so that there will be no earthshaking shock when the amount of petroleum being pumped stops growing.[24] And in this the role of the economist will be crucial, because people, for better or for worse, listen to what economists say about the future.

Unfortunately, the picture that is unfolding in the world of the economy is exactly the opposite of what is needed for stability, or even for survival. Up to about the 1960s the economist was principally interested in growth as a means of ensuring employment and profits. These were, and are, legitimate concerns in capitalist economies, even though if is unclear whether endless growth, even if it were possible, could provide a stable solution. But, as expounded in the previous pages, this has now changed to the more intangible goal of endless growth for growth's sake. To counteract the common-sense view that this would lead to disaster, besides being mathematically impossible, two fantasy-rich theories have appeared in the economic literature since (beginning in the 1960s) environmental problems began to become urgent.

Infinite substitutability

The first of these theories (although not actually a theory in the correct sense, but an article of religious faith) is that human ingenuity will allow any shortages in natural raw materials to be solved by the substitution of synthetic materials. There are myriad natural substances used by human beings, and a few of these have been substituted by artificially produced materials. This substitution has delivered satisfactory results in some cases, and in others (e.g. DDT and the CFCs) has led to or is leading to potentially disastrous consequences. The extrapolation from a few that did go well, to infinity, has led economists to expound the theory of infinite substitutability (see, for example, the statement of J. L. Simon at the beginning of this chapter, that we now have the technology to produce virtually all that we need). There is no basis for this extrapolation, especially since each problem of substitutability must be solved individually.

So much for raw materials, but when one comes to the substitutability of energy sources one runs up against a much stronger obstacle: the First Law of Thermodynamics, a law that even human genius cannot break. Employing another, unutilized, source of energy is not forbidden by the First Law, however. The question is then whether there is such a source available. There is, indeed, an immense amount of unused energy streaming from the sun. But the energy use (and egregious waste) of the present Western society is higher than can probably be met with 'renewables'. It would be technically possible to furnish a society of limited population with all that people really need, with much less energy than is used today. This could be easily done in a totally sustainable way with truly renewable energy from the sun. But that is beside the point. The gist of our thesis here is that an ever-growing energy supply to support endlessly growing production is quite impossible.

Alternative energy sources

Humankind has reached the limit of the utilisation of chemical energy (fossil fuels), and what is left to plunder is energy from the atomic nucleus. There are two possible candidates for this, the fission of certain very heavy elements, and fusion of a tritium–deuterium mixture, both of which processes liberate energy from the atom's nucleus.

A half-century of research and development on the first method, subsidized by taxpayers to the tune of around a trillion dollars, has led to relatively small-scale application: in 2001, 2.7 per cent of the world's energy use was provided by nuclear fission.[25] In addition, there have been a number of accidents with fission reactors, in the case of Chernobyl resulting in widespread radioactive contamination. Perhaps more important is the problem of safe sequestration of deadly radioactive waste, which is, after half a century, as far from solution as ever. But, seen exclusively as a question of an energy source, the most important problem of nuclear power is that the uranium, currently used for nuclear power, is also an exhaustible resource. Very little energy has yet been produced by nuclear power, and very rich ores are still available. But if uranium's use were to increase ten- or twentyfold, the usable ores (i.e. ores rich enough so that the extraction and refining use less energy than is delivered by the nuclear reactors) would be quickly exhausted. There is also an ethical problem with fission to which, by definition, no amount of technical innovation can find an answer: the sibling relationship between nuclear power and nuclear weapons. Since the knowledge of how to make nuclear weapons can never be lost, in order for the use of nuclear energy to be made safe, war would have to be removed from our world. It would take quite a Pollyanna to imagine this happening soon.

There are two fundamental, and fundamentally different, problems with the tritium–deuterium fusion reaction. Firstly, a continuously functioning 'burner' reactor capable of delivering useful energy has yet to be constructed and shown to function reliably for a long period. Secondly, one of the two fuels, tritium, exists only in minute quantities in nature. The solution to the first 'drawback' – that it doesn't work – has, for some 40 years, been predicted every year by protagonists to lie 50 years in the future. The costs of the research show a spectacular growth nonetheless.

As for the second problem, while tritium can be produced by transformation of lithium in a 'blanket' surrounding a fusion reactor by means of a nuclear reaction with the fast neutrons from the reaction, it is not known whether it is technically possible to produce as much as is burned. Whether or not this will ever be possible cannot be known until a working burner that produces useful energy has been built and the whole cycle is tested. The total picture is very reminiscent of the 1950s, when we were told that fast neutron breeder reactors would make more plutonium out of uranium than they would burn. It is unfortunate that in the PR material of the promoters of fusion, lithium is named as the second fuel. This is an evident untruth; it is no such thing. It is, at best, a theoretical source of the real fuel, non-existent tritium.

The upshot of all this is that of the two sources of energy that we are told will replace the fossil fuels that are rapidly being exhausted, one is also based on a resource that would be quickly exhausted if it were to be relied upon for all of society's energy, and the other looks like a pipe dream. An industrial society needs a safe and sustainable source of energy; that is true. Such a source could easily be provided using sunshine, but that supply would not grow infinitely. If we were to put our shoulders to the wheel, such a world could be built, but it would only be sustainable if population growth were to stop and the keyword *save* were to replace the keyword *waste* of today's world. This won't happen until we get rid of both the belief that infinite growth is possible and the belief that an energy supply that can grow infinitely will be found. A further problem is that to be able to manufacture a substitute for any raw material that is in short supply, a large amount of energy will, in general, be needed. If that is not available, it is of no use that a human-made substance can in principle substitute for a depleted raw material.

The 'environmental Kuznets curve' (EKC)

The second defence that was thought up to allay fears that endless growth might irrevocably damage the environment is the idea that *as GNP grows, environmental pollution first gets worst and then, if the GNP gets high enough, improves.* This is generally stated as follows: in the early stages of economic growth, pollution is *coupled* (or *linked*) to the GNP, but at a certain point it becomes *uncoupled* (or *unlinked*), and pollution decreases. This formulation is based on ignorance or misuse of the concept of coupling or linkage. A dependent variable (here pollution) that *increases* when an independent, or 'driving' variable (here GNP) increases is indeed *coupled* (or *linked*) to the independent variable. But if it *decreases* when the independent variable *increases* it is not *uncoupled* (or *unlinked*) from it, but just as *coupled* (or *linked*) to it as in the first case. The coupling or linkage is just functionally different. In discussing this issue it is therefore better to drop the idea of coupling or linkage, and state the hypothesis simply, as in the first sentence of this paragraph. The basic assumption is that as people become richer they become more sensitive to environmental quality and change their behaviour in order to better protect the environment.

Although that was the original assumption, the empirical evidence presented to show that this hypothesis is correct is not based on people's behaviour. This evidence came from measurements of the way the concentrations of some noxious industrial pollutants vary with GNP. These concentrations have been found to diminish in places where the GNP has become relatively large. This is a textbook case of reductionist thinking. If attention is confined to a subset of pollutants, one can say nothing at all regarding the total environmental degeneration caused by a society. To give an adequate answer to the question one would have to correlate GNP with the entire range of environmental effects. To do this quantitatively is an almost impossible task, since it would require (at least partly subjective) assignment of weighting factors to the different sorts of environmental destruction.

One way out of the difficulty in collecting the empirical evidence for and against the EKC hypothesis is to take as a criterion the total energy use of a given country or region, as a reasonable approximation to its total environmental load. In contradiction to the EKC hypothesis, energy use, and thus the total environmental damage, has never decreased, anywhere, with growing GNP. In respect of this, the EKC hypothesis is thus disproved. This argument does leave the question of individuals' 'environmental' response to increasing wealth unanswered, but the answer has been given in a publication by Spangenberg. He presents a detailed study of the many indications that an EKC doesn't exist. In particular he shows that the basic point of departure of the EKC hypothesis is simply wrong, i.e. people do *not* put progressively more accent on environmental services or use their income in more environmentally friendly ways as they become more well-to-do. The relevant section of the paper is as follows.

> If it is true that the consumption pattern of the rich today reflects the aspirations of the majority tomorrow, then – according to this hypothesis – the per capita environmental impact of the rich should be lower than that of the poorer parts of the population, based on the availability and affordably of modern technology with all its efficiency gains. However, if the wealthy people's environmental burden per capita is significantly above the national average, this would indicate a trend towards increasing environmental impact with increasing income, i.e. with growth.

> This has been tested with German data, using an indicator system for environmentally sustainable household consumption.[26] This system, providing a list of the environmentally most relevant consumption patterns, was applied to consumption statistics, disaggregated according to income groups. So the overall environmental impact of different income groups could be compared, again using resource consumption (or environmental space) as an integrated measure.

> . . . Comparing the income group above a monthly net income of 7,500DM (€3,800) to the national average, it turns out that they inhabit flats 30% larger than the average, live in single houses nearly twice as often as the average person, drive significantly longer distances per year, do not use public transport, have more and bigger (i.e. more energy-consuming) cars, fly twice as much (in km) for their holidays.

These findings clearly indicate a significant increase of environmental impacts in the best-earning population group. Consequently, as long as their consumption pattern is shaping public aspirations, increasing wealth will tend to lead to higher resource consumption and thus total environmental impacts.[27]

There is thus no empirical basis for the EKC theory, but instead a solid empirical basis for the hypothesis that as incomes rise, people choose more and more polluting lifestyles. Whatever else there is to say about the effect of economic growth, the *fact* is that increasing GNP leads to more environmental destruction. And, speaking of facts, it is interesting that there are myriad publications in economic journals about the EKC in which the authors do not ask the first question that a simple soul would ask: does it fit the data on total environmental impact as a function of GNP? If it does not, any more words written are a waste of space.

The incurable disease

In this chapter we have expounded upon the forces that are relentlessly driving the rich societies, and with them all of the poor of the world, toward the brick wall at the end of the road of endless growth. Ironically, it is exactly what could have made a pleasurable, stress-free life for everyone possible – the immensely increased *productivity* of labour – that has spun out of control, destroying the health of the biosphere and, in time, perhaps destroying our lives. Earlier we quoted John Maynard Keynes's thoughts on what would be possible for society when the 'economic problem' is solved. His vision of what society, *in principle*, could become is not *a priori* unrealistic.

But the unconventional wisdom of Thorstein Veblen shows us that it is the basic desire to emulate others in unlimited acquisition and conspicuous consumption that has made Keynes's vision unattainable – it is not enough to have much; one must have more than one's peers, and make sure that everyone can see how much one has. For a hundred years now the observations of Veblen have stood like a rock; the only relevant question left is whether there are other societal forces that can be mobilized, in a democracy, to prevent the endless spiral of growth from destroying our world.

A comparison of different periods of recent history can shed light on this question. In particular, if one compares the 1960s with the 1990s one has the impression that one is looking at two different worlds. Just after the Second World War there existed a degree of solidarity that is now unthinkable. Western societies were capable (heavy taxation of the rich made this possible) of providing secure livelihoods to a higher percentage of the population than ever before in history. In Chapter 3 we documented the intense irritation that this caused to the Poppers and the von Hayeks of our world. They fought it tooth and nail, and won their fight. The Thatcher–Reagan era was ushered in and the world will from now on, for at least a long period, not look the same again. The number of well-to-do, rich, very rich and ultra-rich increased spectacularly as a consequence, and the security of the ordinary person decreased steadily. It is still going down, and the bottom is not in sight.

But at the same time, the economic growth that could make the world dreamed of by Keynes possible turned from being a healing medicine into a deadly disease. It is appropriate to end this chapter with a quotation from the work of John Kenneth Galbraith.

> To furnish a barren room is one thing. To continue to crowd in furniture until the foundation buckles is quite another. To have failed to solve the problem of producing goods would have been to continue man in his oldest and most grievous misfortune. But to fail to see that we have solved it, and to fail to proceed thence to the next tasks, would be fully as tragic.[28]

Is this the end of the story? As long as competition is the exclusive hallmark of society, it is. In Chapter 3 we examined the possibility, necessary in our view for a well-ordered society, of balancing competitiveness with solidarity and cooperation. Under the neoliberal flag competitiveness, greed, has got the bit between its teeth – the only slogan one hears is 'Compete aggressively – produce more.' It is clear to us, at any rate, that the extreme predatory behaviour as expressed by this slogan is motivated by greed, an all-too-human characteristic that, as remarked in the Introduction to this book, throughout the ages right up to the advent of the neoliberal world in the early 1970s, has been condemned as dishonourable by all great religions and philosophical schools of thought.

This book is unconventional, in that it is conventionally expected from a writer who criticizes society that he or she will end by saying that there are signs that the situation may improve. To put it bluntly, we see no signs that justify any optimism on this score. The only cause for optimism may be in the actions of civil society, as we will show at the end of this book. In the next chapter we consider the international scene, and there the prospects are, in our opinion, even less encouraging, for the simple reason that powerful nations are not inhibited by rules of decency, or by respect for the opinions of one's peers, as even powerful individuals sometimes are on the national scene.

Chapter 7

Globalization

In this chapter we discuss the distribution of wealth and power, not within nations, but across nations and regions. After the destruction of the Keynesian consensus – the acceptance of Keynesian principles after the 1929 crash – it was but a small step toward the neoliberal (or 'Washington') consensus that signalled the rebirth of the colonial trade regime that had seemed endangered by the flood of decolonization at the conclusion of the Second World War. A number of conditions had to be satisfied in order to make this possible, but the most important one was the 'debt crisis' of the 1970s, which left most poor countries so deeply indebted that they were helpless to defend their own economies. They were thus unable, as we will show in the second part of this chapter, to escape the clutches of structural adjustment (SA) imposed by the World Bank and International Monetary Fund (IMF), that converted this temporary indebtedness into permanent structural inferiority, and through that into persistent powerlessness.

In the eighteenth century the question of whether free trade was good or bad was judged quite differently by economists of a country trying to develop as an industrial society from those of a country seeking to maintain and reinforce its superiority in trade and find new markets for its industrial products. In that period the decision to protect the 'infant industries' of a country could be taken by the country itself, since there was nothing like the World Trade Organization (WTO) to prevent it from doing so. Some countries laid down protective tariff walls that permitted them to achieve, in a very short time, a degree of industrialization and wealth quite comparable with or higher than that of England, the first country to industrialize. With the obvious exception of England, all of the presently powerful industrialized nations were able to become so by providing this protection, in one way or another. The youngest scion of the family is Japan. It maintained an iron-clad defence of its own industry for a long period, but now that it seeks international markets has enthusiastically joined the pack howling for free trade.

Despite its proven efficaciousness as a way to independence, autarky has in modern development discourse become a bad word, and the empirically proven necessity of protecting native industry has been replaced by the completely imaginary necessity of encouraging foreign direct investment (FDI) as the way to develop. Free trade is, in this discourse, a 'good thing' since it promotes the 'integration into the world economy' of the economically weak countries; implying, in contradiction of observable facts, that this integration is a necessary condition for their well-being in the future. A further element of the present consensus development discourse is that development itself is practically synonymous with increase of GNP, and that for poor countries can best be achieved by increasing exports of raw materials and agricultural produce, not by developing a home industrial base. Integral to this view is that development can be measured physically, whereas people are only instruments in the process, not those whose freedom is the goal.

A discourse is more than just the way in which one speaks of a subject; it also circumscribes the actions that are appropriate. In the following we first show how the application of the present discourse maintains developing countries in eternal bondage and tends to destroy their natural resource base – the base that would have been needed to reach a sustainable future, if that future had not already been made unattainable by un-payable debts. A different discourse has been proposed by Amartya Sen.[1] This discourse can be described with the term *freedom discourse*, in which development is seen as an increase in freedom of choice and freedom of action of people and communities. This difference in discourse will be of issue again later in this chapter, when we dissect the meaning of the term 'human capital'.

Freedom and the global economy

The pillar upon which freedom of a country rests is the freedom to control its own economy. The very existence of the WTO is in contradiction with Sen's freedom discourse, since it takes away, from day one, the freedom of every country to do this. It is unfortunate that Sen did not mention this in the otherwise broad discussion in his book of what 'development as freedom' means.

The bitter facts are that with the 'world economy' controlled by the multinational corporations seated in G8 countries (partly directly and partly through their control of the Bretton Woods Institutions [BWI] and WTO), 'integration into the world economy' has become instead a polite euphemism for 'subjugation by the powerful', very far from the freedom at the base of Sen's discourse. The large and increasing flow of wealth from the poor to the rich countries now taking place under this integration regime is well substantiated, even in the publications of the World Bank, which makes it hard not to accuse of hypocrisy those who extol integration as a course leading to universal well-being.

While it is general knowledge that an ordinary bank exists to make the banker rich, there seems to be a remarkable universality of the belief that the World Bank is somehow different – at the very least altruistic, if not overtly benevolent. Such ingenuousness borders on inanity. The fact that the glib term of 'donor nations' is also accepted as an appropriate denomination for the states that supply capital for the loans issued by the World Bank shows how facile repetition can lead to the acceptance as truth of even an obvious falsehood.

Another point of clarification that we must make is that while we speak of 'the rich nations' as if there existed a homogeneous group of equals, this picture is far from reality. For some time now the United States of America has been 'more equal' than the others. This shift in power began immediately after the First World War, and since the end of the Second World War the US has stood alone as the principal capitalist power, with those nations that were its equals in the past reduced to almost vassal status. The BWI (the IMF and the World Bank) were shaped with the specific goal of permanently freezing this status, with the (American) dollar as the eternal world standard of value. Keynes, naive as he was politically, had quite a different vision of peace and justice, and after the Bretton Woods Conference he returned home, visibly disappointed, to die shortly afterwards. Since the Vietnam disaster, however, the status of the dollar has been under pressure because of the financial demands of war-making; this pressure has recently been greatly increased by the American policy of military pre-emption.

Bretton Woods, the World Trade Organization and structural adjustment

The enforcement of 'free trade' on all countries, as a necessary condition for the 'integration into the world economy' mentioned above, began to gather momentum in the 1970s with the Structural Adjustment Programs of the World Bank and IMF. This beginning was followed by further refinement at the conclusion of the Uruguay Round under the rules of the newly created WTO. The consequence is that the presently industrially powerful nations (i.e. the G8) have little fear from competing industrial development of the really poor developing countries. To understand why this is so, it is essential to rid oneself of the illusion that industrialization takes place if factories are built in a country. Industrialization takes place only when native control is maintained over (technical) education, infrastructure and the technologies necessary for industry. If foreign corporations control these factors, one can only speak of neo-colonialism, not of industrialization, since the net result is that the only role that the population plays is that of providing cheap labour while the profits go to the metropolis; that is, to where the investing corporation has its seat. As things stand, it should go without saying that the existence of poverty is a *sine qua non* for the neoliberal model to be capable of reproducing itself.

We should also make it clear that although industrialization has been for some two centuries the key word describing the path a nation must follow in order to reach a position of independence and respect in the world community, it has not led to Valhalla for anyone, and will, unless stopped, and soon, in the end lead to the destruction of even the life-supporting capacity of the biosphere. The reason for this was explained in the previous chapter, as being due to the incompatibility of our preindustrial (or perhaps better, prehistoric) monetary system, which confounds money with wealth, with the finite limitations of the natural world. As shown there, this incompatibility has seduced the rich world into an irrational belief in infinite growth and the accompanying worship of endlessly increasing production. Following this course will finally lead to a collision with the brick wall of exhaustion of resources and destruction of the ecosystem.

But though industrialization, as it is now practised, leads a society in the end into a cul-de-sac, the fact is that unless and until the present development discourse is replaced by something more akin to Sen's freedom discourse, we will have to live in a world where the only way for a nation to achieve control over its own destiny is to industrialize. In contrast, the adoption of Sen's discourse would not only open the way to partnership instead of subjugation but also provide an escape route away from, or around, the catastrophic collision with the physical world that the rich countries are gaily, and apparently blindly, approaching.

The economics profession, with the exception of the ecological economists, is unanimous today in its support of free trade, whereas a century ago this unanimity was lacking. That this unanimity even includes economists in poor countries that only lose by free trade has come about in no small measure through the concentrated drive to recruit promising young economists in developing countries – in particular by the United States – by offering them student scholarships to learn the blessings of neoliberalism. Very few economics professionals rise to influence in a poor country who have not had the advantages of such training in the US or another advanced country, especially since the demise of the Soviet empire. And when they do, they are vulnerable, as is shown by the case of Brazil's erstwhile Secretary of the Environment, José Lutzenberger. He made the fatal error of criticizing a particularly barbarous internal note (leaked to the environmental community) by L. Summers, dated 12 December 1991; at the time Summers was chief economist and a vice-president of the World Bank (he later became President Clinton's Secretary of the Treasury). In this note Summers asserted that the economically correct policy for the disposal of environmental poisons was to dump them in developing countries (which are, in his eyes, severely under-polluted). Lutzenberger wrote to Summers expressing very strong disapproval of these ideas (calling them 'totally insane'), and was removed from his post immediately thereafter. One can guess where the orders came from. The 'pure' economic considerations of Summers are a textbook example of reductionist thinking, which if carried through to actions, have inhuman results.[2]

The specific role of the BWI

The institutional backbone of the new colonialism, as stated above, is formed by the World Bank and the IMF. After McNamara took over the World Bank in early 1968 the loans to poor countries rose spectacularly. These loans were provided for the development of large and gigantic projects, sometimes rammed down the throats of the recipients. These projects had, for the most part, the goal of creating or increasing the export capacity of agricultural or extractive products of poor countries, with the stated purpose (in accordance with development discourse) of increasing their wealth. One would have to be exceptionally naive to believe that McNamara and his fellows at the BWI did not know that this would lead to overproduction and the subsequent collapse of prices on the world market, with the foreseeable consequence that the immense debts incurred in the building up of infrastructure could never be repaid. An additional consequence, attractive for those who control the capital flow of the BWI, is that the inhabitants of the rich countries paid even less than before for the products of poor countries.[3]

It is as if McNamara realized after his years as Secretary of Defense for President Johnson during the Vietnam War that it was extremely difficult to destroy even a small rural country by military force, even if you were militarily the most powerful nation on Earth. Even worse, the attempt to do so would finally meet with devastating opposition on the home front. Upon taking over the World Bank he seems to have changed his tactics: it is much easier to dominate and oppress poor countries by the two-pronged tactic of enticing them to incur large debts with the promise of cornucopia, while simultaneously knocking the bottom out of world markets so that the debts could never be repaid. The tactics were quietly planned in boardrooms so that there was no opposition at home, and no loss of the lives of soldiers. A dramatic description of the sinister motives behind this policy is offered by John Perkins.[4]

The next logical step followed inevitably. The debtor countries were forced to open their doors to imports of manufactured products from the rich countries. This had two results. First there were the profits from sales, and secondly the already impossibly large debts became even larger and hence even more difficult to repay. This is the tactic employed, euphemistically called 'structural adjustment' (loans with conditions attached) in order to give it a nice public face, and it worked like a charm. In the second section of this chapter we examine a case history of what this has meant for one poor country, Costa Rica.

In 1995 James Wolfensohn took over the presidency of the World Bank. He changed the orientation of assistance to developing countries from large infrastructural projects to direct, concrete elimination of poverty. This was welcomed by NGOs working for more effective help for the poor countries, and criticized as 'soft' by most official development assistance agencies. It is unclear whether, in the long run, such a shift can be effective: the crushing debts remain in place, the world markets are not improved by it, and above all, the basic problem of technical independence remains untouched. Added to these difficulties is that Wolfensohn's approach requires a long-term stead-fast adherence to the programme, and the whims of international politics make it unlikely that the US will not prefer a more hard-headed approach. One may not forget that the US determines, in the end, what the BWI may and may not do. In the last instance, as has happened again and again in international organizations, the US can resort to the removal from office of recalcitrant functionaries.

The misperceptions of development assistance

But if the BWI's core task is to hold the poor countries in permanent bondage as providers of cheap labour and cheap products, ironically enough all of the NGOs in the industrialized countries that provide 'development assistance' fight hard to protect the poor countries' right to export agricultural products and raw materials to the rich countries. All those who stand on the barricades to 'protect' the poor countries are unanimous in their insistence that limitations, quotas and tariffs on the industrial and extractive products of the poor countries imported by the rich countries should be eliminated. This sounds noble, and in most instances is born of real desire to help others, but it also testifies to ignorance of the NGO's complicity in maintaining the underclass status of developing countries. If development assistance is ever to increase the freedom of choice (to use Sen's expression) of the poor countries, those well-meaning individuals and organizations must begin to understand that tying the economy to export trade, particularly of raw materials and agricultural products, condemns a poor country to permanent powerlessness and subjugation.

The development NGOs do, indeed, oppose the subsidies given to farmers in rich countries who export products to poor countries, and so they should. These subsidies are morally wrong and should be stopped because they destroy the opportunities of poor country producers to earn, besides the pittance that the world agricultural market offers them for their products, the little bit of pocket money that they otherwise might earn on the home market. Recently this has been frowned upon, and will eventually be stopped.

But at the end of the day, assistance in the build-up of native technical capacity is the only course that can lead to freedom in the world of today, and, as far as we can see, into the world of tomorrow. But unless such a build-up is supported by a policy of autarky, it is doomed to fail because of the overpowering superiority of the already industrialized countries. Start-up industries must be protected against the powerful, in diametrical opposition to WTO policies.

The true face of development

The policy of permanently maintaining poor countries in a lower state of well-being and independence has the same noisome odour as the charity given by Victorian ladies to the deserving poor. It has the same veiled purpose too: namely, that of supporting the status quo by encouraging the poor to stay poor and live on charity – in this case to make sure that the poor countries will never be able to develop a viable industrial base and bootstrap themselves out of poverty. What makes it worse is that the export products are produced by poorly paid workers using modern industrial agricultural methods, frequently on immense tracts of good land that has been bought up by corporations in the metropolis. Native food production is, literally, driven to the edge – to poorer and poorer land on hillsides, while most of the profits from the industrialized agriculture do not go to the people of the country itself but are sent back to the metropolis. Under this regime, initiated by Structural Adjustment Programs 30 years ago, country after country has been forced to begin importing staple foods that it used to grow in sufficient quantities to feed its own people.

A dramatic case in point is that of Mexico, as a consequence of the North American Free Trade Agreement (NAFTA). Mexico is the place on Earth where corn originated. Corn has not only been an important component of Mexico's rural economy, but has also a deep spiritual significance in the people's culture since the times of the Mayas, and even before. Today, as a consequence of NAFTA, almost half of the corn consumed in Mexico is imported from the United States. All of it subsidized, and a major part of it transgenic – that is, genetically engineered. The result has been tens of thousands of peasants having to leave their lands in order to look for non-existent jobs in the large urban areas. Furthermore, local corn varieties have been severely damaged or killed as a consequence of cross-pollination with the transgenic varieties. But the GNP of Mexico has grown one or two points, and that is, according to the neoliberal doctrine, the only thing that really counts.

In the meantime nothing is done, unless with great effort and despite discouragement by those giving 'aid', to build up native technical know-how so that a country can eventually become independent. If the BWI wished to really help poor countries to develop in the sense defined by Sen, they would set up broad programmes to train millions of people in technical skills so that they could not only work in, but run, the industries in their own countries where their own products are made. People would then have the freedom of choice that is Sen's goal of development.

Shadows of the past persist in the present

None of this is new. The English conquerors of India found a blossoming beginning of an industrial revolution. The conquerors destroyed all the machinery they could find, and it was forbidden for Indians to engage in industrial activity. It is time that those in the rich countries who really want to assist their 'dark-skinned' brothers wake up to the reality that we highlighted earlier: globalization is a not just a policy that is bad for poor countries, it is not one iota different from old-fashioned colonialism. The grandchildren of those who spoke so eloquently of their holy (usually 'Christian') duty to elevate the 'dark-skinned white man's burden' from the curse of barbarism up to our level of civilization are today saying that we must help the poor countries integrate into the world market – so that, in effect, their citizens may enjoy the privilege of working in factories or industrial farms owned by corporations in the metropolis for wages so low that they don't have to bother about saving, where trade unions are forbidden so that they don't have to worry their heads about improvement of working conditions, where there are no pesky safety rules to abide by, and where they never have to fill in difficult forms if they have an accident because workers' compensation is unheard of.

We have laid the blame for the present 'development' policies squarely on the doorstep of the investors (where necessary supported by their government) in the metropolis. This is factually correct, but veils an unholy alliance between the rich and oppressive elite who are in the saddle in all poor countries and their counterparts in the metropolis. The 'failure' of nascent democracies in some developing countries was, indeed, directly due to the intervention of the CIA, the task of which is well-described as the subversion of governments of countries of the periphery that threaten to disturb the process of neo-colonization as described in this chapter. On the other hand, it is probable that without the active cooperation of the local elite, some of these interventions might well have failed.

This book has focused on the foundations of the discipline of economics, on the positions taken by mainstream economists, and on the striving of the powerful to protect their position of wealth and power. It would be inappropriate in this chapter, concerned as it is with the trade, power and financial relations between the metropolis and the colonized country, to ignore the important role of the elite of the poor countries in supporting the colonizing policies of the metropolis. They are, of course, royally rewarded for their support. They have more in common with the inhabitants of Fifth Avenue than the latter have with the inhabitants of the South Bronx. Our experience in developing countries is that the elite are proud of this. The local functionaries of the World Bank are also honestly convinced that the bank's policies are beneficial. This could hardly be otherwise, since they generally have close connections with the elite that directly benefits from these policies.

In this account we have made much of the shadow side of the structure of our society, taking a position in direct opposition to conventional wisdom. A reasonable reader has every right to ask for evidence of the consequences for, and in, the poor countries of this world. The following account of the lot of Costa Rica, built largely on independent research, substantiates the picture that we have presented thus far.

What structural adjustment has done to Costa Rica

Costa Rica is uniquely suitable to be examined in this chapter on globalization because on the one hand it is a typical developing country, but on the other it is a special case because it was the first in Latin America to declare that it would shape its policies toward sustainable development. It is therefore highly relevant to see what the BWI policies did to this dream of the future. The president who took office in 1994, José Figueres, reiterated this goal, but if we look at the data of the two previous decades we see that it was already too late to turn the tide. The information presented here is based on the research of Dr Martha Rosemeyer,[5] presented at the International Network of Engineers and Scientists for Global Responsibility (INES) conference in Amsterdam in 1996.

The gathering storm

In the 1970s, Costa Rica suffered severely from the oil crisis and the deflated prices of agricultural products on the world market. It was nonetheless a country that could feed itself and promote a good measure of social justice, in part by imposing tariffs on the importation of luxury goods. It was also unique in that it had eliminated its army – or, to be exact, reduced its military power to a police force of some 6,000 personnel. Table 1 shows the foreign debts of Costa Rica from 1970 to 1991. It is clear that the rising debts were a reason for real concern, and the government turned to the so-called donor nations for relief. This relief was forthcoming (beginning in about 1980), but with the condition, decreed by the BWI, that government spending on health, education and social safety nets should be reduced, and that the economy should be based on exports. The tariffs on luxury goods were removed, and the price supports to farmers producing subsistence crops (rice, beans and maize) eliminated. These measures of reduction of expenditure in the social

Year	Debt	Year	Debt
1970	611	1981	2,829
1971	672	1982	2,851
1972	782	1983	3,554
1973	871	1984	3,380
1974	994	1985	3,584
1975	1,226	1986	3,571
1976	1,428	1987	3,491
1977	1,743	1988	3,202
1978	2,065	1989	2,967
1979	2,335	1990	2,515*
1980	2,529	1991	2,628

* 1 billion dollars forgiven

Table 1. Long-term debt of Costa Rica in $millions (1982). Source: The World Bank, Washington DC, World Tables 1991 & 1994, pp.202-203 & 222-223.

sector (also part and parcel of structural adjustment) had the even more disastrous consequence of destroying the social fabric of a country that had proven itself, left alone, quite capable of enabling all its citizens to live in dignity and security.

The debt figures have been corrected for inflation. If one billion dollars in debt had not been forgiven, the inflation-corrected debt would have risen in 1990 to approximately $3,340 million from the $2,529 million at the beginning of the decade when the SA regime, widely heralded as the way to rid a country of debts, took over.

Structural adjustment destroys the Costa Rican dream

The detailed consequences of these measures are shown in Tables 2 and 3 and Figure 2 (overleaf and page 111). The import of luxury goods, shown in Table 2, went up by a factor of 4.1, in constant dollars, in only nine years. This meant a bonanza for the rich, impoverishment for the common people, and a disaster for the poor. The former could adopt a lifestyle comparable to that of the rich in the USA. The poor farmers, deprived of traditional price supports, lost their land, and either became hired hands on the large cash-crop plantations or were reduced to squatting. The effect of the import of industrial products on the development of home industries is obvious. As we indicated earlier in this chapter, a country can never build a native industrial park unless in the early stages its industries are protected from foreign competition by the government. That has been the history of all industrial nations. The

Luxury goods	1982	1991
Candy	0.3	3.0
Musical instruments	0.3	6.4
Toys	0.8	8.9
Cars	3.7	31.6
Liquor	4.6	5.5
Home furniture and appliances	13.1	38.2
Total	**22.8**	**93.6**

Table 2. The increase in the imports of luxury goods in millions of constant (1982) dollars, after import tariffs were eliminated by structural adjustment measures. Source: Central Bank, Balance of Payments, 1982 & 1991.

policies of the BWI, specifically structural adjustment, and later the dictates of the WTO, are designed to make sure that this will not happen in the developing countries.

Under the SA regime, multinational agricultural corporations take over large areas of the most fertile, level farming areas (in part, the land from which the poor had been evicted) and use highly mechanized farming techniques. The social dimension is partly illustrated by the increase of the police force from 6,000 to 10,500 in the period from 1980 to 1990. There is evidence that this increase was at least in part necessary in order to evict squatters who were desperately trying to cultivate small plots on the edge of the large industrially operated farms.

The financial and social balance

Exports rose spectacularly following implementation of the new policies. There was such a marked growth that in 1991 the World Bank announced that Costa Rica was a textbook case of how SA could make a country rich, and to make it look even better they 'forgave' Costa Rica a billion dollars of the increasing debt incurred in the eighties. The numbers giving the government expenditures in the social sector are shown in Table 3. They look bad, but even these figures do not give the full picture of the human impact of these policies.

	Education	Health	Social	Total
1980	100	100	100	100
1981	101.3	80.9	83.8	87.9
1982	90.6	70.6	90.0	80.4
1983	81.2	66.4	77.5	73.1
1984	81.9	63.0	100	75.4
1985	85.2	64.3	111.3	79.1
1986	85.9	64.3	131.3	82.8
1987	91.9	67.7	153.8	90.3
1988	86.6	67.7	153.8	88.6

Table 3. Index of social sector expenditures as a percentage of government expenditures. The columns for Education, Health and Social show the relative trends of expenditures in the social sector over the period. The Total column is the weighted sum of these expenditures. Source: *Statistical Yearbook for Latin America and the Caribbean, 1990.*

The consequences were spelled out in a report by the Tropical Sciences Centre and World Resource Institute in Washington DC. Costa Rica has been proud of its social programme, which began in 1948 when the army was abolished and educational and social programmes were initiated. The educational programme was spectacularly successful, leading to a literacy rate of 97 per cent. The health care system was so effective that, in this relatively poor country, the infant mortality rate was the second lowest in Latin America.

This all changed in the 1980s. Between 1980 and 1985 the expenditure on education decreased by 30 per cent. This decrease took its toll on enrolment: in primary schools, the enrolment went down 10 per cent and in secondary schools by 5 per cent. The World Bank report, from which the social expenditure figures were taken, states that this "is the most serious cause for concern in the social indicators. It represents a serious deterioration in education which will affect the welfare of individuals and the economic growth potential." In Chapter 6 we saw that while economic growth is a deadly addiction of the rich countries, it is desperately needed by the poor. But the growth brought about by SA improves only the standard of living of the already rich. Unfortunately we have no figures on the effect on health, in particular on the infant mortality rate. The use of prime agricultural land for export crops to the exclusion of subsistence crops, as well as the elimination of subsidies on the latter, led to a shortfall of staple foods, which therefore had to be imported.

These are high prices to pay for the solution to an economic problem, so one must ask whether this problem was actually solved. The supposed goal of SA is to pay off debt by greatly increasing exports. What actually happened is shown in Table 1 (page 106). As mentioned, the spectacular increase in exports was offset by the even more spectacular growth in imports. The luxury-goods dimension of this growth is shown dramatically in Table 2 (page 107). The debt increased by 25 per cent (if one leaves out the one billion dollars that was forgiven), and the trade deficit has continuously increased – and this occurred in the period in which the World Bank proudly announced that Costa Rica was showing the world how a poor country should develop.

Looking back now at the goals of neo-colonialism as described in the beginning of this chapter – e.g. providing cheap labour, agricultural products and raw materials to the benefit of the metropolis and simultaneously providing markets for the metropolis's manufactured goods – one sees that the developments in Costa Rica conform well to this pattern. The luxury imports as shown in Table 2 came, incidentally, almost exclusively from the rich 'donor' countries, directly profiting those who provide the funds for loans. Is it conceivable that their willingness to provide these funds is somehow stimulated by these profits? Frederick Soddy is right to say, as we saw in Chapter 6, that debts do not represent real negative wealth because that does not exist, but for the poor who have to pay them they have a very real human dimension.

The sustainability balance

As mentioned, the exports of Costa Rica increased greatly in the decade of the eighties. These were mainly cash crops. We have already noted that the import of staple foods also increased in this period (later studies show that this was still the case in the second half of the 1990s). To the degree that exports increased, the costs to fisheries, soil and forests increased, in the sense that natural resource depletion took an increasing bite out of the gains. This bite is not financial, and can only be studied by considering and measuring topsoil loss, deforestation, and soil and water pollution, which result in decreased yields. This type of study leads to a correction to the gross agricultural product – a loss factor – and the results of the studies are shown in Figure 2. The losses were never small, but only took a small bite out of the gross agricultural product until the SA programmes, which accentuated export crops, took hold in the 1980s. This loss had grown to about 50 per cent of the total by 1989.

Thus one may conclude that structural adjustment measures, compounding the disaster brought about in the social and economic sectors, also led to an irreversible destruction of the physical basis of the Costa Rican dream of a sustainable society.

Conclusions

It is no exaggeration to say that not only has SA reduced the Costa Rican people to beggars, but it has also led to the destruction of the future possibilities of ever having a sustainable Costa Rica. Once tied to the carousel of the global economy, there seems to be no way to get off. In order to pay its debts,

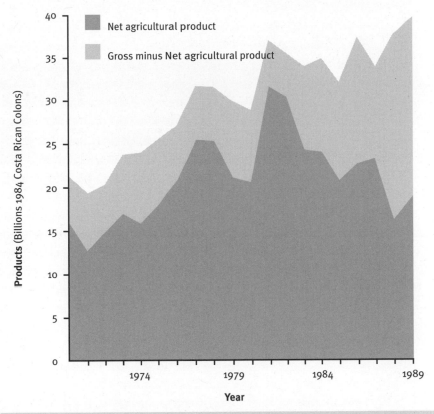

Figure 2. The effect of structural adjustment measures in Costa Rica on the loss of agricultural productivity, as indicated by the increasing gap, after 1980, between the gross and the net agricultural product. Source: derived from data from the *Statistical Yearbook for Latin America and the Caribbean, 1990.*

a country must continually push to increase its exports and reduce its social expenditures. The rich take an increasingly large percentage of the national product and spend it on luxury goods from abroad – as mentioned, principally from the rich countries (and quite obviously to the advantage of the lifestyle of the elite). The downward spiral cannot be stopped because the country becomes totally dependent on credit and cannot possibly step out of this vicious circle without having its economy totally destroyed. In the meantime, the resource base of the country is eaten up so that achieving sustainability, even in the far future, becomes problematic. Once a country has submitted to structural adjustment, it can never free itself again. Repudiating unpayable debts, debts that were specifically constructed under BWI conditions, would lead to reprisals by the BWI that would destroy the country financially. With the advent of the WTO, with even stricter rules, the way back seems blocked forever.

There is a Hindi saying that expresses this well: 'He who rides a tiger can never dismount.'

Development as freedom

The goals of globalization are closely linked in the minds of most people with development. The protests against globalization are in large part motivated by the havoc wreaked on the developing nations, as documented dramatically in the previous section of this chapter, by the globalization of trade and finance. A different goal of development would certainly lead to a different approach to globalization. The goal, *development as freedom*, as envisaged by Amartya Sen, is just such a totally new approach.

At the beginning of this chapter we noted that Sen proposes that development should be thought of in a different way: he advances a different descriptive and normative basis, a different *discourse*, which may be called a *freedom discourse*. This would make it possible to bring about a more human view – and a less 'economic' view – of what development means. We will examine some aspects of this discourse, and in the process dissect the words and phrases employed. In particular we will look at a primary component of 'freedom discourse' and compare it with its counterpart in standard development discourse; this is partly to draw attention to the importance of such an examination in clearing the air of cobwebs of misunderstanding, but more importantly to prepare the ground for the adoption of a more explicitly defined freedom discourse than that espoused by Sen.

Human capital and human capability

In *Development as Freedom* Sen defines the broadening of the freedoms of people to choose the lives they value as the overarching goal of development. It is even imaginable that development as envisaged in the consensus meaning of the term, may not, under the terms of freedom discourse, be called development at all: for example, where wealth production is greatly increased, but under a dictatorship. However, there is a catch here: freedom to make a choice loses its meaning if the actor involved is not *capable* (for any of a great number of possible reasons) of utilizing this choice. Therefore the goal of unfolding and expanding *human capability* (the uncovering or freeing up of suppressed or undeveloped capabilities) is the primary step in the replacement of the consensus definition of development – according to which people are the instruments by which the GNP is increased – by a definition in which freeing human beings is the end goal. This latter view sees development as a human-directed process of achieving freedom, i.e. a humanly, value-driven change in the lives of people.

On this point we are in complete agreement with Sen, but we disagree with his evaluation of *human capital*. In the following discussion it will be seen that there is a close connection between this disagreement and a deeper-lying disagreement on the subject of markets, in particular the labour and land markets. To explain these disagreements, we will first quote Sen's remarks on the difference between speaking of *human capital* and *human capability*. After remarking that the former has recently become more current in economic analysis, compared with the traditional accent on physical capital, he states:

> . . . what, we may ask, is the connection between 'human capital' orientation and the accent on 'human capability' with which this study has been much concerned? Both seem to place humanity at the centre of attention, but do they have differences as well as some congruence? At the risk of some oversimplification, it can be said that the literature on human capital tends to concentrate on the agency of human beings in augmenting production possibilities. The perspective of human capability focuses, on the other hand, on the ability – the substantive freedom – of people to lead the lives they . . . value and to enhance the real choices they have. The two perspectives cannot but be related, since both are concerned with the role of human beings, and in particular with the actual abilities they achieve and acquire. But the yardstick of assessment concentrates on different achievements.[6]

Our view is that the difference is not just a difference of yardsticks but a difference of discourse, in fact a difference between two incompatible worlds of thought. The expression 'human capital' belongs in traditional development discourse where people, just as machines or raw materials, are instruments in production. In the quotation above, Sen weakens his freedom discourse by using a language that is congruent with this instrumental view of human beings, considered as the *means* of achieving higher production, and not the living, breathing, feeling beings whose freedom *itself* is, for Sen, as for ourselves, the legitimate goal of development. We feel sure that Sen would agree with this distinction, and we therefore think that it is unfortunate that he has made use of a compromising formulation.

In order to convincingly deepen the discussion on this point we must digress briefly and bring the work of Karl Polanyi into the picture, especially his treatment of the labour market.[7] Polanyi explains that a basic requisite of a market economy is that all of the elements involved in production and sale be subject to the market, i.e. be available for buying and selling. If this were not the case, the market would not be the sole determinant of the price of commodities, and the basic function of the market could not be realized. In order to carry out this total encompassing of all the elements of production and sale, three non-commodities must be classified as commodities, and traded as if they were.

These non-commodities are land, labour and money – none of which satisfies the characteristic of a commodity that it is produced with the goal of selling it. This is far from an idle distinction. People are not 'produced', so that their labour can be sold on the labour market. In order to be able to speak of the fictitious labour market as if it were just another market, such as the markets for chairs, or for cars or televisions, one has to suppress one's knowledge that labour does not exist as a commodity. It cannot be put on the shelf until sold, but is inseparable from the human being who labours, and who has feelings and thoughts that are a very real part of the world. This separation is monstrously reductionistic. Unfortunately Sen does not acknowledge this basic difference between a real and a fictitious market, and states:

> . . . the rejection of *freedom to participate in the labour market* is one
> of the ways of keeping people in bondage and captivity, and the
> battle against the unfreedom of bound labour is important in many

third world countries today for the same reasons that the American Civil War was momentous."[8] [Our italics]

This quotation indicates that Sen draws the line between unfreedom and freedom at the point where slaves are freed to participate in the labour market, i.e. to sell their own labour instead of it being sold and bought by others. It ignores all of the other human dimensions that one is buying and selling in this fictitious market. Equally important in this exposition is that built into the *market discourse*, as employed in this example by Sen, is another fiction: that all markets are essentially similar in their workings. This is eminently untrue. The worker whose freedom to negotiate is restricted to 'do this or go hungry' is nominally participating in the labour market, but factually enjoys no 'freedom to negotiate'. Unfortunately 'do this or go hungry' is an adequate description of the negotiating freedom of the great majority of non-indentured workers in the world. Quite generally speaking, but especially relevant to the labour market, the 'freedom to negotiate' can only be placed in the category of a substantive freedom when the bargaining power of both sides is approximately equivalent. This is an absolutely basic condition for the title of a 'substantive freedom'. In view of the immense disparity in bargaining power between the individual worker and even a small company, only workers who have the power to engage in collective bargaining through a labour union of their own choice can be spoken of as persons possessing the freedom to negotiate.

Our hesitation to include the labour market in a freedom discourse comes partly from the origin of this market. It did not, nor did standard market discourse, come into being spontaneously. The history of enclosures in England is well known, yet it is not commonly realized that it was the enclosures movement that *created* the labour market in that country on terms, and under conditions, that eminently suited the early capitalists. Free men and women were deprived of their freedom and driven like cattle into the factories. And in our times, the exaltation of the free labour market, as we noted in Chapter 3, was a weapon adopted by von Hayek in his push to destroy the right to collective bargaining – a right won from the powerful by the people in endless conflict, blood and tears. 'Freedom' obviously meant something quite different to von Hayek, Popper and colleagues of the Mont Pelerin Society, from what it means to us. We think (based on many statements of his) that it means the same to

Sen as it does to us, but that he must be more careful in formulating the conditions that must be placed upon negotiation before it can be admitted to the category of substantive freedom. Already, long before the Thatcher–Reagan period, the new discourse was being born and drummed into the public consciousness. We would suggest that Sen's innovative arguments for a different kind of development would be greatly enriched, certainly in clarity of meaning, if his *freedom discourse* were to consider freedom of negotiation on the labour market as being contingent on the presence of labour unions chosen freely by the worker and empowered to bargain collectively.

This would not make the labour market less fictitious, but it would make the lives lived by workers more liveable. This is no small order. The strides in the direction of the right to belong to a labour union and bargain collectively, taken in the inter-war period in rich capitalist countries (only accepted by the powerful because of a certain nervousness caused by the existence of the Soviet Union) have been destroyed in recent decades by the ascendance of neoliberal economic theory and practice. In the rest of the world, developments in this direction have not even begun to get off the ground. In a great majority of countries, murdering labour leaders, although not openly condoned, is a common sport of the powerful.

The land market: buying and selling life itself

What is true of the labour market is even more true of the land market and of nature in general. Nature has an infinite number of dimensions, only one of which can be bought and sold. Land can in no way be considered a marketable commodity, simply because it is not produced by humankind to be sold; nor will its amount increase if the price per hectare rises, or diminish if the hectare price goes down. It is the heritage of all humankind today, and of all future generations tomorrow. It cannot be 'owned', any more than one can own the stars, the sun and the moon.

In another, real, sense the inclusion of land in the market is even worse than marketing labour. The worker can, in combination with his fellows, defend him- or herself to some degree from the greed of his employer. Nature cannot do this, and the environmental destruction and resulting loss of vitality of the ecosphere (for example the loss of biodiversity), seemingly inherent in our civilization, may be an omen of disaster. It is interesting to note that, long before the world became aware of environmental problems, Polanyi foresaw what the land market would lead to.

> Nature would be reduced to its elements, neighbourhoods and land-scapes defiled, rivers polluted, military safety jeopardized, the power to produce food and raw materials destroyed.[9]

The heritage of the land market that the present and preceding generations are leaving for our descendants will complete the process Polanyi describes, unless those in power wake up to truths that so-called primitive peoples apparently understood long ago. The present globalization of markets is wreaking havoc on nature. This destruction currently has little impact on those in the rich countries, but since environmental destruction will finally also become global, it will not remain far from any of us forever.

Some thoughts on markets in general

From what we understand from his writing, Sen does not distinguish between real and fictitious markets, and he sees the fictitious labour market as a positive example. He uses an analogy to speak of the role of markets.

> To be *generically against* markets would be almost as odd as being generically against conversations between people (even though some conversations are clearly foul and cause problems for others – or even for the conversationalists themselves). The freedom to exchange words, or goods, or gifts does not need defensive justification in terms of their favourable or distant effects; they are part of the way human beings live and interact with each other (unless stopped by regulation or fiat). The contribution to economic growth is, of course, important, but this comes only after the direct significance of the freedom to inter-change – words, goods, gifts – has been acknowledged.[10]

In responding to this we encounter a difficulty, because one proves nothing using analogy as a method of argument: one usually succeeds only in cloud-ing the issue, and this is certainly true of the quotation above. Conversations between people are part of our evolutionary heritage, built into our DNA, and the exchange of gifts is older and of an entirely different nature from the exchange of goods. Markets have been created – they do not just happen – in order to satisfy certain societal needs or desires; more often than not to establish or buttress a difference in status (as in the example earlier of the enclosures movement in England). These differences are of kind, not degree.

We are not *generically against* markets. But surely Sen must recognize that the deregulation and privatization since the 1980s (to the tune of the one endlessly repeated buzzword, the 'market mechanism') have had disastrous effects on humanity, and, more important for the main message of this book, have been enthusiastically supported by almost the entire economics profession. Sen's failure to place *a priori* restrictions on his praise of the market, and in particular his unequivocal endorsement of the freedom to negotiate on the labour market as constituting a substantive freedom, is a great disappointment. There are basic conditions that must be satisfied before 'negotiation on the labour market' can be called a substantive freedom.

Sen has made gigantic steps toward humanizing economics. That we have expressed unvarnished criticism of one aspect of his thinking does not diminish our admiration and respect for him. And, naturally, we hope that such criticism as ours will provoke him to distance himself even farther from mainstream economics. Whatever he says or does from now on, even the Bank of Sweden cannot take his well-deserved Nobel prize away from him.

Conclusion

We end this chapter with another quotation from the opening speech of the late Prince Claus of the Netherlands at the 20th conference of the Society for International Development, May 1991.

> Perhaps, Ladies and Gentlemen, we must await the appearance of a 'green' Keynes to help us out of this predicament. But preferably a Keynes who is born in and belongs to the 'South'.

Chapter 8

Compassion

Why this chapter?

The greatest part of this text has been occupied with demonstrating that the economic profession has for the most part, in theory and in practice, dedicated itself to defending the injustices in our society: in particular the poor–rich divide, with all its inhuman consequences for the lives of the less fortunate members of the world community. The destruction of Keynesianism and the propagation of the neoliberal view of the world has been the most recent manifestation of this inherent goal of the profession, a principle rooted in the class division described 500 years ago by Machiavelli and cited in the first paragraphs of Chapter 2 of this book. We have pointed out that while the economic profession as a whole has always stood solidly behind this defence of class structure, there have been several dissenting voices. One of the most distinguished was the economist de Sismondi, who cried out in anguish against the misery and injustice wrought on the lives of the workers, the wealth-producing segment of mankind, by the economic policies – in particular 'free trade' or laissez-faire – that provided in his day the intellectual backbone of the justification of social injustice, just as it today performs the same function for neoliberalism. It was his human compassion, and not so much his intellectual prowess, that singles him out from the rest, and provides us with the one shining example of how economics as a discipline could have, perhaps under different circumstances, developed. This chapter is dedicated to his vision of a world made liveable by justice.

De Sismondi published several books; the one from which we have taken the most of our inspiration is *Nouveaux principes d'économie politique* (*New Principles of Political Economy*). This was published in two editions, the first appearing in 1819 and the second seven years later. It has been translated into

English very competently by Richard Hyse, who also provides an exhaustive commentary.[1]

Value premises

The reader will remember that in Chapter 4 we argued that in general the value of the social sciences would be greatly increased if there were a cultural shift toward the social scientist clearly stating his or her value premises. This is normally not done, partly because such a practice would undermine the pretension that the social sciences are (like physics is supposed to be) value-free. The following quotation from the beginning of Book 1 of de Sismondi's *New Principles*, entitled 'The Double Goal of the Science of Government', expresses in no uncertain terms the value premises built into de Sismondi's work.

> The object of government is, or ought to be, the happiness of men united in society. It seeks the means of securing to them the highest degree of felicity compatible with their nature, and at the same time of allowing the greatest possible number of individuals to partake in that felicity. In none of the political sciences should one lose sight of this double goal of the legislator. He has to care at one and the same time for the degree of happiness that mankind may attain through social organization, and the equitable participation of everyone in that happiness. He has in no way accomplished this task if, in order to assure equal enjoyment of happiness to all, he makes it impossible for outstanding individuals to develop fully, if he permits no one to rise above his peers, and if he does not offer anyone as a model to mankind, and as a guide to discoveries which will benefit everyone. He has not achieved it any better if, having no other goal than the improvement of these gifted individuals, he raises a small number above their fellow citizens at the price of suffering and degradation of all others. . . . That nation is enslaved where the great mass of people is exposed to constant privation, to painful anxiety about its existence, to anything which will suppress its will, corrupt its morals, stain its character, even though it may count among its upper classes newly successful men who have achieved the highest degree of happiness, whose every ability has been developed, whose every right is guaranteed, whose every enjoyment is assured.

When, on the other hand, the legislator does not lose sight of the development of the few as well as the happiness of everyone, when he succeeds in organizing a society in which individuals can achieve the highest perfection of spirit and soul, as well as the most sensitive enjoyments, but in which at the same time all members are assured to find protection, education, moral development, and physical comforts, then he has fulfilled his task; and without a doubt, this is the noblest task a man may set as his goal on this Earth. In pursuing this sublime end the science of government represents the loftiest theory of welfare. It cares for individuals collectively as well as individually. It protects all those whom the imperfections of our institutions have rendered unable to protect themselves.

Yet, nothing is more common in all of the political sciences than to lose sight of one or the other aspect of this double goal. On one side the passionate lovers of equality rise against any type of distinction: in evaluating the prosperity of a nation they compare at all times its total wealth, the sum of its rights, its total knowledge, with the share of each, and the gap they find between the powerful and the powerless, the well-to do and the poor, the idler and the worker, the educated and the ignorant, brings them to the conclusion that the sufferings of the latter are monstrous faults in the social order. If those on the other side, who always look merely in the abstract at the goal of human effort, find guarantees for various rights and means of resistance, as in the republics of classical antiquity, they call that order liberty, even though it is founded on the slavery of the lower classes. If they find an inventive spirit, deep thoughts, as in France before the Revolution, they see in that social system a high degree of civilization, even though four-fifths of the nation cannot read, and all provinces are immersed in deep ignorance. If they find a tremendous accumulation of riches, an improved agriculture, a prosperous business community, manufactures which multiply without end all products of human industry, and a government that disposes of almost inexhaustible coffers, as in England, they call the nation opulent that has all of these things, without stopping to inquire *whether all those who work with their hands, all those who create this wealth*, are not reduced to mere subsistence; whether every tenth member among them must not apply each year to the public welfare; and whether three-fifths of all individuals, in a nation that is called rich, are not exposed to more privation than an equal proportion of individuals in a nation called poor.

The association of men in a political body could not take place formerly, and cannot be sustained even today, for any other reason than the common advantage they derive from it. No law can be established among them if it is not founded on that trust which they have reciprocally extended to each other, contributing to the same end. The system continues to exist because the overwhelming majority of those who belong to the body politic see in the system their security; and the government exists only to provide, in the name of all, the common benefit everyone expects of it. Thus, the many benefits, unequally divided in society, are safeguarded by society because from that very inequality flows advantage to all. The means to bring some individuals to the highest possible excellence, the means to turn such individual excellence to the greatest common benefit, the means to save all citizens from suffering, and to prevent that anyone should be hurt by the play of passions and the pursuit of self-interest by his fellowmen, all of these varied objectives make equality a part of the science of government, since all of them are equally necessary in the development of the national happiness. [Our italics]

A greater lucidity in the declaration of one's ethical principles concerning the proper goals of the state is hardly imaginable. De Sismondi does not hide the pitfalls and potential contradictions in a too-radical interpretation (in his view) of the position he takes. He saw injustice clearly, but was apparently unable to formulate clearly a Keynesian answer to the contribution of unregulated markets to gross social injustice, and the role that the government could have in ameliorating this. De Sismondi recognized, without making a great deal of it, as is shown by the phrase we highlighted in italics in the third paragraph of the foregoing quotation, that it is the worker who creates wealth; or, more generally stated, wealth is created by human effort. Adam Smith considered it quite normal that the worker live in a state of 'mere subsistence', although his attitude regarding the justice or injustice of this situation is quite different from de Sismondi's.

By agreeing with the value premises of de Sismondi we clearly distance ourselves from the traditional role of economics in its defence of social injustice. But what has this to do with the 'scientific' discipline of economics? In our view the connection is not only intimate but of the essence. In Chapter 2 the connection was summarized, and in Chapter 3 the extraordinary callousness of the 'father' of neoliberalism, Friedrich von Hayek, regarding human suffering was discussed at length as an example of a 'conscienceless' social science.

A deeper difference between the mainstream perspective and ours is that the traditional scholar is brought up with the conviction that a 'real' science is totally divorced from human feeling, whereas we quite shamelessly advocate that any social science worthy of the name is built first upon human convictions and sentiments. We realize that by taking this unequivocal position we distance ourselves from the Newtonian picture of science – in the minds of most scholars the foremost symbol of unemotional scholarship, i.e. 'real science'. So be it! As we have already remarked, the usefulness of social science as a study that, if it is worth its salt, has the intrinsic goal of improving the lot of mankind, has been seriously degraded since the middle of the nineteenth century by the adoption of mathematical formalism and Newtonian thinking, in an ineffective and actually rather ludicrous attempt to divorce itself from the stain of being considered 'unscientific'.

Economics too could be a useful tool in improving the lot of humankind if it could divorce itself from these same degrading influences, and, to begin with, from every vestige of utilitarian thinking that only forms an obstacle to the acceptance of the multiple dimensions of human happiness. The 'needs and satisfiers' matrix of Max-Neef (see Chapter 10) forms a realistic basis for mature thinking about human satisfaction. In no way does it neglect the physical and animal needs of all beings, but places them in the total picture, much as is apparent in the quotation on the previous pages by de Sismondi.

De Sismondi: a revolutionary in economics

De Sismondi was in some respects a very conservative thinker, but as regards justice he was extraordinarily radical. His work was the object of scorn on the part of thinkers of the school of Say and Ricardo; his sober empiricism demonstrated a clean break from the fantasies built into the economic theories of these two very highly acclaimed economists. Both claimed that more production automatically led to more consumption, and that therefore a glut of goods in the market was impossible. This is too absurd a standpoint to withstand a moment's examination. In the 1820s such gluts were common, and led to hitherto unexposed suffering of the working class. This kind of blindness to reality, this acceptance of the truth of theory as being more real than reality when theory does not conform to the world about us, seems to be widespread among economists. In our days we have seen interest rates reduced to record lows with the stated intention of awakening economic revival, without having the theoretically predicted effect at all. For years on end the Chairman of the Federal Reserve, Alan Greenspan, kept lowering the interest rate, apparently in no way losing his faith in a theory that at best is based on faulty reasoning.[2] And when it finally got as low as it realistically could, the Chairman, apparently devoid of any more bright ideas, simply left it there. The constructions of Say and Ricardo were equally inadequate, and also failed totally to connect to reality.

De Sismondi quotes a disciple of Ricardo who tries to justify Ricardo's standpoint on the basis of a make-believe world constructed by Ricardo's disciple that, not surprisingly, behaves as Ricardo says the real world does. De Sismondi's comment on the quote is deadly.

> There is perhaps no other method of reasoning that is open to more errors than that of constructing a hypothetical world altogether different from the real one, in order to use it for one's hypothesis. The mind, already confused by the impossibilities that are part of the hypothesis, can no longer distinguish those that imply contradictions, and which, as a consequence will render the argument false.[3]

The logical objections of de Sismondi to the nonsense of Ricardo and Say had no effect whatsoever on the world of economists. The reason is that the ideas of Ricardo and Say translated the preferences of the wealthy (in this case, the lack of any feelings of fellow humanity toward the workers).

It is certainly not our intention to imply that Ricardo and Say were responsible for the injustices of society, but simply to show that their ideas added intellectual fuel to the arguments of the privileged who profited from, and consequently defended, that injustice. Just as Say and Ricardo were not directly responsible for the injustice of their times, it would hardly be fair to blame the impoverishment of the middle and lower classes that accompanied the vast enrichment of the wealthy and ultra-wealthy and the fatal wounding of the fabric of society brought about by the total triumph of greed – the great success story of neoliberalism – on Friedrich von Hayek or Milton Friedman. At the same time, it is undeniable that their status contributes to the acceptability and the glory of this relatively new religion. It is thanks to them that the worship of murderous competition and the icon of endlessly increasing production have gained respectability – a status unreachable, for clear ethical reasons, in earlier stages of civilization.

De Sismondi, pleader for social justice

As we have seen, the world in which de Sismondi lived was a far cry from the world he envisages in the introductory remarks in the passage quoted on page 120 from 'The Double Goal of the Science of Government'. His social instincts prompted him to do what he could to rectify this injustice. For this, he was accused of rather awful things, essentially because he attacked the status quo. His real views as a social reformer are made clear in the following quotation from the second article of the appendix to the second edition of *New Principles*.

> I hear already complaints that I am opposed to the improvement of agriculture, to advances in the trades, to all progress man is capable of; that without a doubt I prefer barbarism to civilization since the plough is a machine, that the spade is an even older machine; and that, according to my method, it would have inevitably happened that man would cultivate the soil with his hands alone.

I have never said anything of the kind, and I demand leave to protest, once and for all, against any consequences inferred from my method which I have not deduced myself. I have not been understood by those who attack me, nor by those who defend me, and more than once I have had to be ashamed of my allies as well as my opponents. I have been pictured as being, in political economy, the enemy of society's progress, a supporter of barbarous and oppressive institutions. No, I do not desire any part of what has been, but I want something better of what is. I cannot judge what that is, except by comparing it with the past, and I am far from wanting to restore ancient ruins if I show with their help the eternal needs of a society.

I beg to pay close attention – it is not in any way against machines, against inventions, against civilization that I raise my objections, it is against the new organization of society which, by taking away from the working man all property except his arms, gives him no guarantee against a competition, a mad auction, conducted to his disadvantage, and of which he must necessarily be the victim. Let us assume that all men share equally the product of their labour in which they will have cooperated; then every invention in the trades will, in all possible instances, be a blessing for all of them; because, after every advancement in industry, they will always be able to choose, either to have more leisure with less labour, or to have with the same labour more pleasures. Today, it is not the invention that is the evil; it is the unjust division man makes of its results.

We are, and this has as yet not been sufficiently noticed, in an entirely new state of society, one of which we have as yet no experience whatsoever. We incline to separate completely any type of property from all types of labour, to break all ties between the worker and his employer, to exclude the former from all participation in the profits of the latter. This organization is so new that it is not even halfway instituted, such that only the most industrialized, the richest, the most advanced countries belong to a system we have barely tried out, where agricultural labour, as well as that in the manufactures, will be performed by workers who can be dismissed at the end of every week; this is the road we will follow; this is where I call attention to danger, and not in the inventions of science.

Our senses have become so accustomed to this new organization of society, to that universal competition which degenerates into hostility between the wealthy class and the working class, that we cannot imagine anymore any other type of existence, even of those whose ruins lie about us everywhere. One believes one can answer me with absurdities, by holding up to me the vices of the preceding systems. Two or three systems have actually succeeded, with respect to the status of the lower classes of society; but, they do not deserve our regret, because after having done first a bit of good, they then imposed frightful calamities on humanity. Can it then be concluded that we have today attained to the truth? that we will not discover the fundamental evil of the day-labour system, as we have discovered the evils of slavery, of serfdom, of guilds? When these three systems were powerful, nobody imagined, in the same way, what would come afterwards: rectifying the existing order would have seemed similarly either impossible or absurd. The time will undoubtedly come when our descendants will judge us not any less barbarous for having left the working classes without security, as they will judge, and as we judge ourselves as barbarous, those nations who have reduced the same classes to slavery.[4]

We have in this chapter brought our story regarding what is wrong, in the human sense, with the discipline of economics to a logical end. The following chapters, after analysing the neoliberal breakdown of 2008-9, will deal with some of the conditions that a new economics, coherent with the challenges of the twenty-first century, should fulfil.

Chapter 9

The world on a collision course and the need for a new economics

In October 2008, at the same time that the Food and Agriculture Organization of the United Nations (FAO) was informing us that hunger is affecting 1 billion[1] people, and estimated that $30 billion annually would suffice to save those lives, the concerted action of six central banks (USA, EU, Japan, Canada, United Kingdom and Switzerland) poured $180 billion into the financial markets in order to save private banks. The US Senate approved an additional $700 billion, and two weeks later another $850 billion. That not being enough, the rescue package continued to grow, until by September 2009 it had reached an estimated $17 trillion.

Facing such a situation, we are confronted with two alternatives: to be a demagogue or a realist. If, based on the law of supply and demand, we say that there is a greater demand in the world for bread than for luxury cruises, and much more for the treatment of malaria than for haute couture; if we propose a referendum asking citizens if they prefer to use their monetary resources to save lives or to save banks; we will be accused of being demagogues. If, on the contrary, we accept that it is more urgent, more necessary and more convenient and profitable to all to prevent an insurance company or a bank going bankrupt rather than feed millions of children, or give aid to victims of a hurricane, or cure dengue fever, it will be said that we are realists.

This is the world in which we find ourselves: a world under the spell of a dehumanized economy, as we have shown in the preceding chapters, and hence a world accustomed to the fact that **there is never enough for those**

who have nothing, but there is always enough for those who have every-thing. After the events we witnessed during 2009, the obvious question arises: Where was that money? For decades we have been told that there are not enough resources to overcome poverty, yet there are more than enough resources to satisfy the wants of speculators. $17 trillion divided by the $30 billion the FAO estimates to be enough for overcoming world hunger – instead of saving private banks – could generate **566 years of a world without hunger**. Would not a world without misery be a better world for everyone, even for the banks?

What are we facing in our world today?

The quadruple convergence[2]

We are facing many challenges, the most important of which are enumerated below.
1. An exponential increase of human-induced climate change affecting all regions of the world.
2. The end of cheap energy, which will have dramatic effects on societies.
3. The extensive depletion of key resources basic to human welfare and pro-duction, such as fresh water, genetic diversity, forests, fisheries, wildlife, soils, coral reefs and most elements of local, regional and global commons.
4. The gigantic speculation bubble, which is 50 times larger than the real economy of exchange of goods and services.

The root causes of this convergence are:
1. The dominant economic paradigm, which encourages rapid economic growth at any cost and stimulates corporate greed and the accumulation of wealth.
2. The uncontrolled use of fossil fuels to feed that obsessive economic growth.
3. The promotion of consumerism as the road to human happiness.
4. The decimation of traditional cultures in order to impose conventional economic industrial models; this brings about the loss of cosmologies, languages and values that differ from those of the dominant culture.
5. The disregard of planetary limits in relation to resource availability, con-sumption, waste generation and absorption.

6. Over-population: the eventual growth of population beyond the sustainable capacity of the Earth.

These conditions may bring about unprecedented dangerous environmental and social costs:

1. Climate chaos and global warming imply the loss of much productive land, storms, rising sea levels, massive dislocation of peoples, desertification and, especially in poorer countries, economic and social problems.
2. The depletion of inexpensive oil and gas supplies will have a direct impact all over the world, threatening future industrial development. It will make it increasingly difficult to operate industrial food systems and urban and suburban transportation systems, as well as to produce many commodities basic to our accustomed way of life, such as cars, plastics, chemicals, refrigerators, etc. All these are predicated on the availability of an inexpensive and ever-increasing energy supply.
3. Other resource shortages such as of fresh water, forests, agricultural land and biodiversity; we are facing the possible loss of 50 per cent of the world's plant and animal species before the end of the century.

Crisis or crises

What we are facing today is not simply an economic and financial crisis but a crisis of humanity. It is probably true to say that never before in human history have so many crises converged and peaked at the same time. To the economic and financial crisis we can add increasing corruption in the spheres of politics, economics, religion and sports; the consolidation of greed as a fundamental value; gigantic enterprises exclusively concerned with their own benefits; judicial systems that forget justice; an obsession with growth at any cost; the destruction of nature and disdain for planetary limits; the decadence of education and health systems; hyper-consumerism; hyper-individualism; global warming; climate change; the eagerness for power; and the disdain for life. These are colossal convergences that can only result in equally colossal outcomes.

If we are to find solutions to these converging problems, we need new models that, above all else, begin to accept the limits of the carrying capacity of the Earth. We must move from *efficiency* to *sufficiency and well-being*. Also necessary is a resolution of the present economic imbalances and inequities, for without equity peaceful solutions are not possible. We need to replace the dominant values of greed, competition and accumulation with those of solidarity, cooperation and compassion.

This paradigm shift requires a turning away from economic growth at any cost and a transition towards societies (especially in the rich countries) that can adjust to reduced levels of production and consumption, and, in the case of developing nations, that stimulate localized systems of economic organization. We need once again to look to the local rather than to the global marketplace.

Before we can make this shift, however, we need to understand why the dominant economic model has become so strongly ingrained in our world and in our everyday life.

The myths that sustain the dominant model[3]

To sustain a model, arguments are required. What follows is a series of arguments for the dominant economic model. They are generally presented as self-evident, but in fact they are no more than myths.

Myth 1: 'Globalization is the only effective route to development'

Between 1960 and 1980 the majority of developing countries, especially in Latin America, adopted the principle of 'import substitution', which allowed for significant industrial development. This principle was the same as that applied in the early nineteenth century by countries such as Germany and the United States in order to defend their infant industries against the might of the English industrial colossus. In fact, all the rich countries of today attained their development by applying the same principle. In eighteenth-century Britain, Adam Smith himself was inclined in the same direction: Chapter 2 of Book Four of his *Wealth of Nations* is entitled 'Of Restraints upon the Importation from Foreign Countries of such Goods as can be produced at Home'. In fact, it is in that same chapter that one finds the only sentence of the entire treatise where he mentions 'the invisible hand'; and he mentions it precisely in an argument favouring import substitution.

By preferring the support of domestic to that of foreign industry, he intends only his own security; and by directing that industry in such a manner as its produce may be of the greatest value, he intends only his own gain, and he is in this, as in many other cases, led by an invisible hand to promote an end which was no part of his intention.[4]

From 1960 to 1980, per-capita income in Latin America grew by 73 per cent and in Africa by 34 per cent. After 1980, economic growth in Latin America came to a virtual halt, increasing on average by not more than 6 per cent over 20 years, while growth in Africa declined by 23 per cent.

In the period from 1980 to 2000, import substitution was replaced by deregulation, privatization, the elimination of international trade barriers and a full openness to foreign investment. The transition was from an inward-looking economy to an outward-looking one. From our analysis of statistics from the United Nations Development Programme (UNDP), the World Bank and the Economic Commission for Latin America and the Caribbean (ECLAC), we can show that the poorest countries went from a per-capita growth rate of 1.9 per cent annually in the 1960–1980 period to a decline of 0.5 per cent a year between 1980 and 2000. The middle-income group of countries did worse, dropping from an annual growth rate of 3.6 per cent to just under 1 per cent after 1980. The world's richest countries also showed a slowdown.

Countries such as South Korea and Taiwan, frequently cited as examples to be emulated, achieved their development, so to say, in the old manner: that is, through trade barriers, state ownership of the big banks, export subsidies, violation of patents and intellectual property, and restrictions on capital flows including on direct foreign investment. It would be absolutely impossible for any country to replicate these strategies today without severely violating the regulations of the World Trade Organization (WTO) and the International Monetary Fund (IMF). According to the present rules, poor countries must remain poor.

Myth 2: 'Greater integration into the world economy is good for the poor'

Poor countries must adapt to a number of rules and restrictions established by the international organizations. The result is that poor countries divert human resources, administrative capacities and political capital away from more urgent development priorities such as education, public health and industrial capacity.

In 1965, the average per-capita income of the G7 countries was 20 times that of the seven poorest countries. In 1995 it was 39 times larger, and today (2011, the G7 having become the G8) it is over 50 times. In practically all developing countries that have adapted to a rapid trade liberalization, income inequality has increased. In Latin America, real incomes have declined by 20-30 per cent.

More that 80 countries have today a lower real per-capita income than they had one or two decades ago. The paradox is that it is precisely these more marginal countries that have integrated themselves more completely into the global economy.

Myth 3: 'Comparative advantage is the most efficient way to ensure a prosperous world'

One of the unquestioned principles of modern politics is the need for global free trade: to doubt its benefits is an act of heresy. However, in spite of its supposed greater efficiency as compared with other systems of economic organization, global free trade is notoriously inefficient in real terms. By giving greater priority to large-scale production for export purposes instead of small- and medium-scale production for local needs, and by generating competitive pressures that put communities into conflict with other communities the world over, the prices of consumer products may decrease, but at at enormous social and environmental costs.

There is still a dominant belief in the benefits of adhering to comparative advantages. However, according to the model of David Ricardo (the creator of the concept) the system functions as long as there is no transnational mobility of capital. Internally, capital searches for the most adequate niche that gives it a comparative advantage. However, when capital is granted full trans-national mobility, it will look for *absolute* advantages. As John Gray says:

> When capital is (transnationally) mobile it will seek its absolute advantage by migrating to countries where the environmental and social costs of enterprises are lowest and profits are highest. Both in theory and practice, the effect of global capital mobility is to nullify the Ricardian doctrine of comparative advantage. Yet it is on that flimsy foundation that the edifice of unregulated global free trade still stands.[5]

For example: the Nike Corporation (footwear manufacturer) needs to reduce its costs in order to remain competitive. So, it moves to Indonesia where, through independent contractors, the shoes are made by young girls who are paid around $0.15 per hour. The reality is described by David Korten.

> Most of the outsourced production takes place in Indonesia, where a pair of Nikes that sells in the United States and Europe for $73 to $135 is produced for about $5.60 by girls and young women paid as little as fifteen cents an hour. The workers are housed in company barracks, there are no unions, overtime is often mandatory, and if there is a strike the military may be called to break it up. The $20 million that basketball star Michael Jordan reportedly received in 1992 for promoting Nike shoes exceeded the entire annual payroll of the Indonesian factories that made them.[6]

Myth 4: 'More globalization means more jobs'

According to the International Labour Organization (ILO), in 2000 there were 150 million unemployed around the world and 1 billion under-employed – making up one third of the world's workforce. And, the ILO says, the situation is deteriorating.

The *outsourcing* as described in the previous section (Myth 3) is a necessity of the big corporations in order to remain competitive. It goes without saying that such a process generates unemployment in the place of origin, and under-employment in the country to which the work is outsourced, owing to the extremely low salaries and miserable working conditions.

Myth 5: 'The World Trade Organization is democratic and accountable'

> Many decisions affecting people's daily lives are being shifted away from local and national governments and are instead being made by a group of unelected trade bureaucrats sitting behind closed doors in Geneva. They are now empowered to dictate whether the EU has the right to ban the use of dangerous biotech materials in the food it imports, or whether people in California can prevent the destruction of their last virgin forests, or whether European countries have the right to ban cruelly trapped fur."[7]

According to the rules of the WTO, if a transnational corporation investing in a given country concludes that there are certain national laws or regulations considered to be inconvenient to its interest, the country is forced to abolish them, or adapt them to the satisfaction of the investor. This means that under WTO rules, the race to the bottom (described in Myth 3) is not only in social and environmental standards but also in democracy itself.

The WTO has no rules whatsoever about child labour or workers' rights. Everything in its constitution is shaped to the advantage of corporations. For instance, during the discussions that gave rise to the WTO, known as the Uruguay Round, the controversial issue of intellectual property rights was put on the agenda by 13 major companies, including General Motors and Monsanto. In the negotiations that followed, 96 of the 111 members of the US delegation working on property rights were from the private sector. It is unsurprising that the final agreement serves corporate interests and undermines poor people's access to knowledge and technology. This is strikingly illustrated by the fact that poor countries are not allowed to produce their own inexpensive generic pharmaceutical products but are forced to buy the ones produced, at much higher prices, by the pharmaceutical corporations. The consequences have been particularly tragic in the case of HIV in Africa, where corporate prices are far beyond the purchasing power of the great majority of the suffering population.

In short, the WTO should be recognized for what it really is: an institution whose main purpose is to enable the corporations to rule the world.

Myth 6: 'Globalization is inevitable'

Renato Ruggiero, former Director General of the WTO, used to say that "trying to stop globalization is tantamount to trying to stop the rotation of the Earth". Bill Clinton pointed out that "Globalization is not a political option; it is a fact." Tony Blair identified globalization as "irreversible and irresistible". Margaret Thatcher proclaimed that "there is no alternative" to free-market capitalism. All such statements are an evidence of the degree of fundamentalism of the defenders of the system. As such, the model amounts to a pseudo-religion.

Alternatives are certainly possible. The point is that the dominant model has been the product of the systematic renunciation, on the part of the majority of countries, of their right to control economic processes for their own benefit. Yet any condition that originates in political decisions is obviously reversible.

It will most probably be argued that any change would mean a choice between the present economic rules on the one hand and chaos on the other. This is of course absurd. A fundamental change could be an increased relocalisation of the economy at local levels, designing new rules that bring production and consumption closer to each other, and giving rise to what we like to call a human-scale economics.

Human-scale economics

The most important contribution of a human-scale economics is that it may allow for the transition from a paradigm based on greed, competition and accumulation to one based on solidarity, cooperation and compassion. Such a transition would allow for greater happiness not only among those who have been marginalized but also among those responsible for this marginalization, despite what they may believe.

The parameters for a human-scale economics could include the following:
1. The use of local currencies, so that money flows and circulates as much as possible in its place of origin. It can be shown by economic models that

if money circulates at least five times in its place of origin, it may generate a small economic boom.

2. The production of goods and services as locally and regionally as possible, in order to bring consumption closer to the market.
3. The protection of local economies through tariffs and quotas.
4. Local cooperation in order to avoid monopolies.
5. Ecological taxes on energy, pollution and other negatives. At present we are taxed on goods and not on 'bads'.
6. A greater democratic commitment to insure effectiveness and equity in the transition towards local economies.

The long and unethical evolution of the discipline of economics, which has been expounded in this book, must come to a stop. A new economy needs to be created in order to overcome all the inequities of the present dominant model.

Alternative schools of thought are emerging – from Post-Keynesianism to Evolutionary and Behavioural Economics, Institutional Economics, Ecological Economics and Econophysics – but are not yet sufficiently developed to provide a definitive alternative to neoliberalism. We shall not go into the description of each of these schools of thought, but rather propose that all alternatives in the making, no matter what their final theoretical structure might be, should integrate the principles of a human-scale economics. These principles are expressed in five postulates and one fundamental value principle, all of which are compatible with any new alternative. They are as follows.

Postulate 1. The economy is to serve the people, not the people to serve the economy.

Postulate 2. Development is about people, not about objects.

Postulate 3. Growth is not the same as development, and development does not necessarily require growth.

Postulate 4. No economy is possible in the absence of ecosystem services.

Postulate 5. The economy is a sub-system of a larger and finite system, the biosphere; hence permanent growth is impossible.

Value principle. No economic interest, under any circumstances, can be above the reverence for life.

The dominant economic model today is largely based on the polar opposites of these five postulates. Yet it is absurd to assume that an economy based on the above postulates would not be feasible, for it is already being practised in many countries at the local, regional and municipal levels – the Swedish movement of Eco-Municipalities being a conspicuous case in point.

In the following chapters we will go deeper into the meaning and implications of each of these postulates.

Chapter 10

A humane economics for the twenty-first century

This chapter outlines the foundations of what we consider a new economics, coherent with the problems of the twenty-first century, should take into consideration.

Postulate 1: The economy is to serve the people, not the people to serve the economy

The effects of outsourcing (as described in Myth 3 of the previous chapter) are a clear case of humans being used for economic interests. Any corporation that outsources its production according to the principles consecrated by the WTO produces unemployment in its place of origin and under-employment in the place where the work is outsourced. A great many examples of this could be listed.

More shocking is the issue of child and slave labour. It is unbelievable that today, in the twenty-first century, there are more slaves than there were before the abolition of slavery in the nineteenth century, at least two-thirds of these being children. The fact that such a situation does not even reach the news reveals the degree of perversity that the dominant economic model has been able to impose.

As noted by David Sirota: "Those of us pushing for serious trade policy reform have argued for years that businesses are aiming to create global economic policies that allow them to trawl the world for the most exploitable forms of labor. As General Electric CEO Jack Welch famously said, corporations want laws that allow them to 'have every plant you own on a barge' – one that can move from country to country looking for the worst conditions to exploit. Such an international economic regime would (and now does) allow the worst governments to create artificial comparative economic advantages through bad/immoral policies."[1]

Global business has so far opposed every effort to put labour, environmental and human rights standards into the so-called 'free-trade agreements', and is doing everything in its power to weaken the laws barring products made with child slave labour. They know that the fewer rules that exist, the more cost-cutting exploitation they can engage in; for them, that is what 'good business' is all about.

Postulate 2: Development is about people, not about objects

A detailed discussion of this postulate is contained in my (Manfred's) book *Human Scale Development*,[2] so it is useful to include an extensive quotation from that text here.

> The acceptance of this postulate leads to the following fundamental question: How can we determine whether one development process is better than another? In the traditional paradigm, we have indicators such as the Gross Domestic Product (GDP) that is in a way an indicator of the quantitative growth of objects. Now we need an indicator of the qualitative growth of people. What should that be? Let us answer the question thus: The best development process will be that which allows the greatest improvement in people's quality of life. The next question is: What determines people's quality of life? Quality of life depends on the possibilities people have to adequately satisfy their fundamental human needs. A third question arises: What are those fundamental human needs, and/or who decides what they are?
>
> It is traditionally believed that human needs tend to be infinite, that they change all the time, that they are different in each culture or environment and that they are different in each historical period. It is suggested here that such assumptions are inaccurate, since they are the product of a conceptual shortcoming.

A prevalent shortcoming in the existing literature and discussions about human needs is that the fundamental difference between *needs* and *satisfiers* of those needs is either not made explicit or is overlooked altogether. A clear distinction between both concepts is necessary.

Human needs must be understood as a system: that is, all human needs are interrelated and interactive. With the sole exception of the need of subsistence, that is, to remain alive, no hierarchies exist within the system. On the contrary, simultaneities, complementarities and trade-offs are characteristic of the process of needs satisfaction.

We have organized human needs into two categories: existential and axiological, which we have combined and displayed in a matrix. [See Table 4, page 143.] This allows us to demonstrate the interaction of, on the one hand, the needs of Being, Having, Doing and Interacting; and, on the other hand, the needs of Subsistence, Protection, Affection, Understanding, Participation, Idleness, Creation, Identity and Freedom.

From the classification proposed, it follows that food and shelter, for example, must not be seen as needs, but as satisfiers of the fundamental need of Subsistence. In much the same way, education, study, investigation, early stimulation and meditation are satisfiers of the need for Understanding. Health schemes may be satisfiers of the need for Protection.

There is no one-to-one correspondence between needs and satisfiers. A satisfier may contribute simultaneously to the satisfaction of different needs or, conversely, a need may require various satisfiers in order to be met. For example a mother breastfeeding her baby is simultaneously satisfying the infant's needs for Subsistence, Protection, Affection and Identity. The situation is obviously different if the baby is fed in a more mechanical fashion where only the need for Subsistence would be satisfied.

Having established a difference between the concepts of needs and satisfiers it is possible to state two additional postulates. First: *Fundamental human needs are finite, few and classifiable.* Second: *Fundamental human needs are the same in all cultures and in all historical periods. What changes, both over time and through cultures, are not the needs, but the way or the means by which the needs are satisfied.*

Each economic, social and political system adopts different methods for the satisfaction of the same fundamental human needs. In every system, they are satisfied (or not satisfied) through the generation (or non- generation) of different types of satisfiers. We may go as far as to say that one of the aspects that defines a culture is its choice of satisfiers. Whether a person belongs to a consumerist or an ascetic society, his/her fundamental human needs are the same. What changes is his/her choice of the quantity and quality of satisfiers. In short: *What is culturally determined are not the fundamental human needs, but the satisfiers for those needs.* Cultural change is, among other things, the consequence of dropping traditional satisfiers for the purpose of adopting new or different ones.

It must be added that each need can be satisfied at different levels and with different intensities. Furthermore, needs are satisfied within three contexts: a) with regard to oneself (*Eigenwelt*); b) with regard to the social group or community (*Mitwelt*) and c) with regard to the environment (*Umwelt*). The quality and the intensity, not only of the levels but also of contexts, will depend on time, place and circumstance.

It should be the purpose of every political, social and economic system to generate the conditions for people to adequately satisfy their fundamental human needs. This is a paramount condition for a new economy to be coherent with the problems of the twenty-first century.

The matrix presented, in which needs are invariant and satisfiers can change as much as necessary, is only an example and in no way exhausts the number of possible satisfiers.

The proposed needs perspective . . . allows for the reinterpretation of the concept of poverty. The traditional concept of poverty is limited and restricted, since it refers exclusively to the predicament of people who may be classified below a certain income threshold. This concept

Needs/satisfiers matrix

	Being (qualities)	Having (things)	Doing (actions)	Interacting (settings)
Subsistence	physical, emotional and mental health	food, shelter, work	work, feed, procreate, clothe, rest/sleep	living environment, social setting
Protection	care, adaptability, autonomy	social security, health systems, rights, family, work	cooperate, plan, prevent, help, cure, take care of	living space, social environment, dwelling
Affection	respect, tolerance, sense of humour, generosity, sensuality	friendships, family, relationships with nature	share, take care of, make love, express emotions	privacy, intimate spaces of togetherness
Understanding	critical capacity, receptivity, curiosity, intuition	literature, teachers, educational and communication policies	analyse, study, meditate, investigate	schools, families, universities, communities
Participation	adaptability, receptivity, dedication, sense of humour	responsibilities, duties, work, rights, privileges	cooperate, propose dissent, express opinions	associations, parties, churches, neighbourhoods
Idleness	imagination, curiosity, tranquillity, spontaneity	games, parties, spectacles, clubs, peace of mind	day-dream, play, remember, relax, have fun	landscapes, intimate spaces, places to be alone, free time
Creation	imagination, boldness, curiosity, inventiveness, autonomy, determination	skills, work, abilities, method, techniques	invent, build, design, work, compose, interpret	spaces for expression, workshops, audiences, cultural groups
Identity	sense of belonging, self-esteem, consistency	symbols, language, religion, values, work, customs, norms, habits, historical memory	get to know oneself, grow, commit oneself, recognize oneself	places one belongs to, everyday settings, maturation stages
Freedom	autonomy, passion, self-esteem, open-mindedness, tolerance	equal rights	dissent, choose, run risks, develop awareness, be different from, disobey	temporal/spatial plasticity (anywhere)

Table 4. Matrix of needs and satisfiers. It should be noted that the matrix does not contain any material elements. So, in the 'Having' column there are no objects; only principles, institutions, norms, traditions, etc. In conventional economics we have two links: wants and goods. In Human Scale Development Theory (see Chapter 13) we have three links: needs, satisfiers and goods. For instance, there is the need for Understanding, whose satisfier is literature and whose good is a book.

is strictly economistic. It is suggested here that we should speak not of poverty but of poverties. In fact, any fundamental human need that is not adequately satisfied reveals a human poverty. Some examples are as follows: poverty of subsistence (due to insufficient income, food, shelter, etc.); of protection (due to bad health systems, violence, arms race, etc.); of affection (due to authoritarianism, oppression, exploitative relations with the natural environment, etc.); of under-standing (due to indoctrination instead of education); of participation (due to marginalization and discrimination of women, children and minorities); and of identity (due to imposition of alien values upon local and regional cultures, forced migration, political exile, etc.). But poverties are not only poverties. Much more than that, *each poverty generates pathologies*. This is the crux of our discourse.[3]

The discourses of power are full of euphemisms. Words no longer fit with the facts. Annihilators are called 'nuclear arms', as if they were simply a more powerful version of conventional arms. We describe a world full of examples of the most obscene inequities and violations of human rights as 'the free world'. We call the most colossal system of exploitation 'free trade', as elaborately documented in this book. Examples could fill many pages. The end result is that people cease to understand and, as a consequence, either turn into cynics or into impotent, perplexed and alienated masses.

We may draw the following conclusions:
1. Any fundamental human need that is deeply unsatisfied in terms of intensity and duration generates individual pathologies.
2. Today we find increasing examples of collective pathologies due to inequities, violence and injustices affecting parts of or complete societies.
3. The understanding of these collective pathologies requires transdisciplinary research and action.

New collective pathologies are being generated, and will continue to be in future if we maintain the traditional and orthodox approaches. The discipline of economics, in becoming increasingly reductionist and technocratic, has given way to a process of dehumanization. To humanize ourselves again from within our own economic discipline is the great challenge. Only such an effort can build the foundations for a fruitful endeavour that may truly contribute to solving the predicament in which we find ourselves today.

We need a sense of responsibility for the future of humanity and a strong desire to overcome all the inequities described in this book. If we do not take up the challenge, we will be accomplices in creating and maintaining sick societies.

Postulate 3: Growth is not the same as development, and development does not necessarily require growth

It is generally assumed that the more an economy grows, the more successful it is. The main indicator is of course the Gross Domestic Product (GDP), on the basis of whose behaviour political decisions are made. It represents the flux of goods and services that are traded in the market through producers and consumers, measured in monetary terms.

GDP has a number of shortcomings, which are normally not taken into consideration when it comes to policymaking. First, everything is added, regardless of whether the impacts are positive or negative. The costs of traffic accidents and of diseases are included, just as are investments in infrastructure and education. There is no difference between goods and bads. Second, GDP does not include the value of unpaid work, thus discriminating against household and voluntary work that is fundamental in a society. Third, GDP considers only that which can be expressed in monetary terms. Fourth, nature and ecosystems services are given no value at all.

Considering such limitations, it is obvious that no real assessment of quality of life or welfare can be made using the GDP. If we accept what has been proposed in Postulate 2, that development is about people and not about objects, and that that development is best where the quality of life improves the most, we must look for a different indicator, an indicator that will disaggregate GDP into two accounts: a national benefits account and a national costs account.

A number of studies that examined alternative methods more accurately evaluating quality of life were carried out by myself (Manfred) and colleagues some 20 years ago in different countries, using the Human Needs Matrices (as in Table 4, page 143) in order to assess quality of life and/or welfare. In the process certain unexpected evidences began to show up, which led us to propose what we called the 'Threshold Hypothesis' which states that: "*In every society there is a period in which economic growth contributes to an improvement of the quality of life, but only up to a point, the threshold point, beyond which if there is more economic growth, quality of life may begin to deteriorate.*" A few months after we proposed the hypothesis, based on our qualitative analysis, a study was published by Daly and Cobb (1989)[4] in which a new indicator, called an Index of Sustainable Economic Welfare, where positives and negatives are disaggregated, was proposed. Applied to the United States for the period 1950-1990, it shows a parallel increase with GDP up to 1970, and a decline after that year despite a continuous increase in GDP.

As a result of our proposed hypothesis and the Daly and Cobb study in the USA, a number of groups were organized in different countries to repeat the studies using the same methodology. The threshold began to appear in practically all cases, provoking a great debate between a number of economists. Several of them dismissed the findings as methodological errors, while others made constructive suggestions in order to improve the index.

After 20 years, improvements have been made and the indicator has changed name, becoming the Genuine Progress Indicator. Many more studies have been carried out, in most cases confirming the threshold. Although there are still some economists who dismiss the results, the majority seems to be positively inclined. It can at least be stated that, at this stage, the Threshold Hypothesis is a robust hypothesis that has become fundamental in the field of ecological economics. Results for eight countries can be seen in Figure 3.

If we accept that the Threshold Hypothesis is coherent with reality, some significant changes should be expected in development theory.

The fundamental question is: how does the economy function before the threshold point, and how does it function after the point? Much analysis is still required, but a few assumptions can already be made. For instance, if there is poverty in a country that has not reached its threshold, it is legitimate to point out that in order to overcome poverty more growth is necessary. However, after the threshold has been reached such an argument no longer

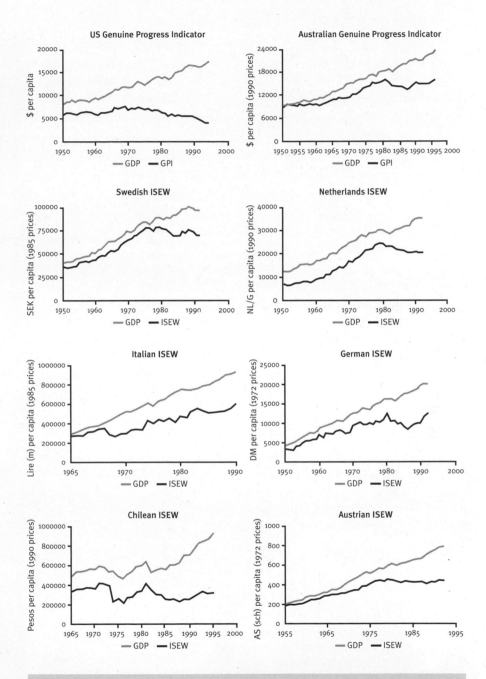

Figure 3. Index of Sustainable Economic Welfare / Genuine Progress Indicator for selected countries. Source: Friends of the Earth.[5]

holds, because the economy has reached a point in which the costs of growth outweigh the benefits. In the language of ecological economics, defensive expenditures become dominant, and economic growth becomes uneconomic growth. Hence the overcoming of poverty must be the result of specific policies addressed to the purpose, since growth alone can no longer do the trick. We can identify the pre-threshold period as a quantitative economy and the post-threshold as a qualitative economy. Economic laws that function in one segment no longer function in the same way in the other segment. Much is still to be investigated in order to fully understand the characteristics of post-threshold economies.

Postulate 4: No economy is possible in the absence of ecosystem services

It is disturbing that 'economics' that is still being taught in most universities represents a closed system that has no relations with any other system. It is just a flow of goods and services through the market and between firms and families, expressed in monetary terms, that has no relation to the environment, and ignores the physical impacts and consequences of economic activity.

As a matter of fact, if one goes through the index at the end of any of the most important textbooks of economic theory, words such as 'ecosystem', 'biosphere', 'nature' and 'thermodynamic laws' are nowhere to be found.

Figure 4 represents the conventional vision of the economy.

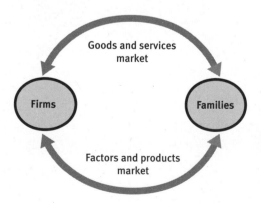

Figure 4. The classic approach to the economic process. This shows a circular flow of money in a closed system that does not have a relationship with the environment and ignores the physical consequences of the economic activity.

Figure 5 represents the economy as interpreted and understood according to ecological economics.

The economy depends on services provided by the biosphere, such as the supply of energy and materials, the capacity to absorb residues and the maintenance of biodiversity; at the same time it produces impacts on the biosphere in terms of dispersed energy, degraded materials, pollution and residues, global warming and, as a consequence, climate change. This being the case, it is high time that economists develop a systemic vision of economic processes and their relationship with all those components of the biosphere that are responsible for the maintenance of life.

There are ten planetary boundaries[6] – limits that should not be surpassed – all of which are affected by economic activity. They are: climate change, rate of biodiversity loss, the nitrogen cycle, the phosphorus cycle, stratospheric ozone depletion, ocean acidification, global freshwater use, change in land use, atmospheric aerosol loading and chemical pollution. Of these ten boundaries, three have dangerously crossed their acceptable limits. Regarding *climate change*, the proposed boundary of carbon dioxide concentration

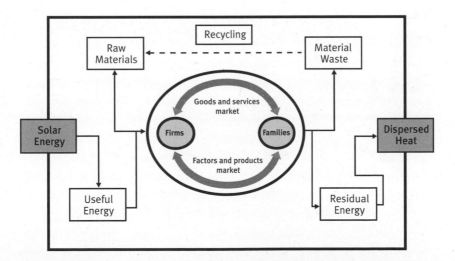

Figure 5. The ecological economics approach. This shows the economy as a subsystem of a larger and finite system, the biosphere, from which all ecosystem services derive. These are services without which no economy can be possible.

(parts per million by volume) is 350. The current status is 387, while the pre-industrial value was 280. Regarding *biodiversity loss*, the proposed boundary for extinction rate (number of species per million species per year) is 10. The current status is over 100, while the pre-industrial rate was 0.1-1. Regarding *the nitrogen cycle*, the proposed boundary for the amount of N_2 removed from the atmosphere for human use (millions of tonnes per year) is 35. The current status is 121, while the pre-industrial amount was 0. The remaining boundaries are slowly approaching their limits as well.

This being the case, it is inconceivable that such fundamental conditions for the maintenance of life, deeply affected by economic processes, are totally absent in the economics curricula. This is the result of the absurdity that in the twenty-first century, facing problems that have no historical precedent, we are still teaching nineteenth-century economic theories as if there were no alternatives – hence the large number of economists who create marvellous abstractions with their economic models but do not understand the real world in which we are living. We will say more about this in Chapter 12.

Postulate 5: The economy is a sub-system of a larger and finite system, the biosphere; hence permanent growth is impossible

Sustainability is essentially a matter of scale. That means that we must accept that we have only one finite planet, within a biosphere that is also finite. If, in addition, we recognize that anything and everything we produce can be reduced to an amount of land necessary to produce it, the question that must be answered is: What amount of ecologically productive land area do we need in order to support the resource demands and to absorb the wastes of a given population or specific activities? This is called the 'ecological footprint' of the population in question; detailed analysis and calculations reveal that in order to maintain the resilience of our planet, we must not go beyond 1.8 hectares per person. Yet, as Figure 6 shows, since 1986 we have crossed that threshold and are now using the resources of one-and-a-third planets. This means, among other things, that it takes nature 16 months to regenerate the renewable resources that we use in 12 months. That is obviously not sustainable.

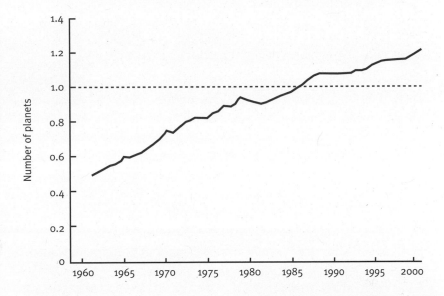

Figure 6. Humanity's ecological footprint. The footprint tracks the consumption and waste patterns of individuals, communities, businesses and nations, showing that we now overuse our planet's natural capital by up to 25%. See www.footprintnetwork.org.

Despite this evidence, which is known to economists, we continue with 'business as usual'. No doubt the great Kenneth Boulding was right when he said:

> Those who believe that economic growth can go on forever in a finite planet are either mad or are economists.

Not only the ecological footprint shows that we are already overdrawn. If we evaluate economic processes in terms of energy units rather than monetary units, we reach similar conclusions. We know what the land budget per person is, and we now need to know what the energy budget per person should be.

Searching for the answer, I (Manfred) proposed years ago the name Ecoson (acronym of ECOlogical perSON) for the per-capita energy budget. At the time it was not clear to me how to calculate it. The answer came from German physicists Ziegler[7] and Dürr[8] who, using the loss of biodiversity as a consequence of human impact on a given ecosystem as an indicator for environmental over-stress, suggested a *critical value of anthropogenic primary energy flow per unit area and time* of about

14 +/- 2 GJ/km²/day = 160 +/- 20 kW/km²/day = 0.16 W/m²/day

which should not be surpassed. An appropriate extrapolation shows that an anthropogenic world-throughput of primary energy of 9 terawatts per day is the limit in order not to exceed the carrying capacity of the biosystem of the Earth. Nine terawatts amounts to 20 per cent of the natural flow of the sun's energy that goes through the Earth's biosystem.

If we divide 9 terawatts by 6 billion planetary inhabitants, what we get is:

1 Ecoson = 1.5 kW/pp/h or 13,000 kW/pp/yr

which is the energy budget per person that should not be surpassed in order not to exceed the carrying capacity of the biosystem.

The main importance of establishing the Ecoson is that we can reconceptualize some demographic considerations. If we classify all countries according to their per-capita income, what we get is shown in Table 5.

The first line shows all countries with per capita annual income below US $1,000, which amounts to 390 million people yet using only 13 million Ecosons, meaning that those inhabitants are far below the 1.5 kW per person per hour energy budget. The first three lines represent countries with more people than Ecosons. In the next three lines the situation is reversed, and we have countries with more Ecosons than people. The country with the greatest

Income	Population (thousands)	Ecosons (thousands)
-1,000	390,000	13,000
1,000-1,999	1,370,000	274,000
2,000-3,999	1,920,000	1,152,000
4,000-7,999	840,000	1,624,000
8,000-15,999	240,000	528,000
+16,000	760,000	3,851,000

Table 5. World population grouped by per capita income, showing the number of Ecosons for each section of the population.

gap between people and Ecosons is the United States: with 300 million inhabitants it uses almost 4 billion Ecosons.

What is the importance of all this? It can be explained in very simple terms: the baby just born in Boston Central Hospital is not equivalent to the baby just born in a hut in Sierra Leone. They are not equivalent because their impact on the biosphere will be dramatically different. In fact, the impact of one American baby may be equivalent to that of 10 or 15 Sierra Leone babies. Hence, if we are concerned with sustainability, it is much more important to know the number of Ecosons for each country, because they represent the true impact of the population. To illustrate how dramatic this new way of understanding demography is, Table 6 shows the true size of the United States in comparison with other countries in Ecoson terms.

	Ecosons (thousands)	Relative size of the USA
USA	1,938,956,000	
India	206,540,000	9.4
China	696,591,000	2.8
Indonesia	56,973,000	34.0
Brazil	99,224,000	19.6

Table 6. The real size of the United States.

In terms of population size, India and China are much bigger than the United States. But when seen from the perspective of ecological economics, the United States, with its 300 million inhabitants, is nine times bigger than India, three times bigger than China, and so on. For those who favour population control, the message should be to control not people but Ecosons.

The calculations reveal that 6 billion Ecosons is the maximum global energy budget if we are not to upset the carrying capacity of our biosystem. According to available statistical information, the present global energy consumption amounts to 8 billion Ecosons. Hence, just as in the case of our ecological footprint, here again we find an overdraft of 30 per cent; that is, we are living as though we had 1.3 planets, although we have only one.

If our concern is sustainability, evaluating economic processes in terms of energy instead of money is much more revealing.

Value principle: No economic interest, under any circumstances, can be above the reverence for life

No examples of this principle are necessary. The degree to which this fundamental principle is systematically violated is so overwhelming that one can only hope that if our culture's insistence on having more of the same kind of economics brings about the gigantic catastrophe that seems likely, a dramatic cultural shift may then occur that would lead us from an anthropocentric world of greed, competition and accumulation to a biocentric world of solidarity, cooperation and compassion with all forms of life.

Chapter 11

The United States: an underdeveloping nation

What may surprise many people concerned with development problems is that injustices and inequities brought about by the neoliberal economic ideology do not only affect the citizens of the poorer nations of the world, as described in earlier chapters of this book, but those of the rich countries as well. The model is, in fact, designed to work against the people, wherever they are, with the sole exception of the mega-rich and the mega-powerful. In the United States there are millions of people who suffer as much as the most vulnerable people in other poverty-stricken areas of the world.

The development discourse recognizes three types of country: underdeveloped, developing and developed. For decades these categories have seemed sufficient for descriptive and comparative purposes. However, under the present circumstances it seems desirable to consider a fourth category: that of *underdeveloping* countries – those going from better to worse – of which the United States is without doubt the most conspicuous example.

Since 1970 the quality of life and the economic conditions of the immense majority of Americans, with the exception of the top financial elite, has steadily deteriorated.[1] The US is the most unequal of all the advanced economies, with the coexistence of enormous wealth and extreme poverty. It is the richest nation in history, but also has the highest poverty rate in the industrialized world. Fifty million US citizens are living in poverty. For at least three decades there have been wage stagnation, mounting poverty and attacks on the social welfare system. Wealth redistribution has occurred, but only towards a tiny financial elite through the massive bailout designed to save the financial speculation industry.

The unpalatable facts

The impoverishment of US workers during the current economic crisis has been documented by a report from the Northeastern University, which analysed unemployment in 2009, based on income data for the previous year.

> Unemployment in the fourth quarter of 2009 for those at the bottom 10 per cent of household earnings was at a Depression level of 31 per cent. A broader measure of unemployment, the labour market under-utilization rate – which combines unemployment, underemployment, and those who have fallen out of the workforce because they have ceased actively searching for work – was over 50 per cent among the bottom decile of earners; for the second decile, 37.6 per cent; and for the third and fourth lowest income deciles, 17.1 per cent and 15 per cent respectively. For the top 10 percent of earners, the underutilization rate was 6.1 per cent. The data is indicative of 'a true Great Depression', according to the report, yet there was no market recession for America's affluent.
>
> The sharp polarization that reveals itself in fabulous wealth for a handful, on the one hand, and unemployment, wage cuts, homelessness and hunger for a broad layer of working people on the other, marks an intensification of longer-term trends.
>
> According to the Economic Policy Institute: 'While many middle-income families have lost jobs, homes, and retirement savings during the latest recession, their economic woes date back much further.' In the 30 years before 2008 – the onset of the current crisis – nearly 35 per cent of total income growth in the US was cornered **by the top one-tenth of 1 per cent of income earners**. The bottom 90 per cent shared only 15.9 per cent of income growth in the same period.[2]

We may also add a pretty scary list of conditions that prevail in the United States today, and that may become a permanent feature as long as the neo-liberal model continues to be the basis for the mainstream economy:[3]

1. 50 million people need food stamps to eat.
2. 50 per cent of US children will use food stamps to eat at some point in their childhoods.
3. 20,000 more people need food stamps every day.
4. In 2009 one out of five households didn't have enough money to buy food. In households with children, the number rose to 24 per cent.
5. 50 million citizens are without health care.
6. The US has the most expensive health care system in the world, with citizens paying twice as much as in other countries, while the overall care they get in return ranks thirty-seventh in the world.
7. 1.4 million Americans filed for bankruptcy in 2009, a 32 per cent increase on 2008.
8. Americans have lost $5 trillion from their pensions and savings since the economic crisis began, and $13 trillion in the value of their homes.
9. Personal debt has risen from 65 per cent of income in 1980 to 125 per cent today.
10. Five million families have already lost their homes, and 13 million families are expected to lose their homes by 2014.
11. Every day 10,000 homes enter foreclosure.
12. An increasing amount of people are not finding shelter elsewhere, amounting to three million homeless Americans.

One place where more and more Americans are finding a home is in prison. The prison population is 2.3 million, which means there are more people incarcerated than in any other nation in the world. For every 100,000 citizens in the US there are 700 imprisoned. In contrast, for every 100,000 citizens China has 110 imprisoned, France has 80 and Saudi Arabia has 45. The US prison industry is thriving. A recent report from Hartford Advocate titled 'Incarceration Nation' reveals that a new prison opens every week somewhere in America.[4]

What is really disturbing is that this kind of information never reaches the news, so the picture offered by the authorities is always deceptive. Unemployment is a case in point. The official figures don't count people who are 'involuntary part-time workers'; that is, people who are working part-time but want a full-time job. It also doesn't count 'discouraged workers', meaning long-term unemployed people who have lost hope and have ceased to look for work. All these people are taken out of the unemployment figures.[5] The paradox is that instead of the number of unemployed rising, the official news will report that unemployment is levelling off. And this, of course, will generate a very favourable reaction in Wall Street, to the benefit of the top earners.

Economic inequality, poor quality of life

We mentioned at the beginning of this chapter that conditions have been deteriorating in the United States since 1970, turning it into the most unequal of all the advanced economies. This should be evident from what has been described so far, but the picture is further reinforced by the behaviour of the US Gini coefficient (a measure of the inequality of income or wealth) over time.[6] The figures below are from the US Census Bureau.

> 1929: 45.0 (estimated)
> 1947: 37.6 (estimated)
> 1967: 39.7 (first year reported)
> 1968: 38.6 (lowest index reported)
> 1970: 39.4
> 1980: 40.3
> 1990: 42.8
> 2000: 46.2
> 2005: 46.9
> 2006: 47.0 (highest index reported)
> 2007: 46.3
> 2008: 46.6

It can be seen from these figures that 1970 is the starting point of the negative trend. If this is compared with the Genuine Progress Indicator (GPI) for the US (Graph 1 of Figure 3, page 147), which begins to decline in 1970, some conclusions must be drawn. While the Gini coefficient increases, the GPI decreases. That is, the more income inequality increases, the more quality of life deteriorates. And at this point in time, the Gini coefficient of the US is among the worst 23 per cent of the world.

The fact that the only segment of the US population that has constantly improved its lot is the top one per cent, at the expense of the other 99 per cent, can be seen from additional figures. In 1970 CEOs made $25 for every $1 the average worker made. By 2000 the ratio had risen dramatically: $90 for CEOs to $1 for the average worker. However, if stock options, bonuses and other benefits are included, CEO pay is actually $500 to the worker's $1. The total combined wealth of the 400 richest Americans amounts to $1.57 trillion, which is more than the combined net worth of 50 per cent of the US population. In the US, 400 people have more wealth than 155 million combined.[7]

The scandal of the top earners

But what we consider the most monumental scandal was revealed by the US Internal Revenue Service in December 2009. The information received little attention until February 2010, and refers to income and taxes of the 400 top-earning families. Their average income – denominated in 1990 dollars – grew between 1990 and 2006 from $17 million to $87 million, representing a five-fold increase in real terms (see Figure 7).

During that period, the percentage of the total national income that went to

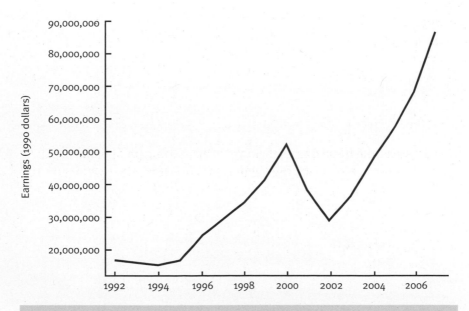

Figure 7. Average income of top-earning 400 US families.

the top 400 families tripled, from 0.52 per cent in 1992 to 1.59 per cent in 2007 (see Figure 8).

The data shows that the income of these families increased by 31 per cent just between 2006 and 2007, the average income for each family being $345 million dollars. As far as the taxes they paid are concerned, they fell from 30 per cent in 1995 to 16.6 per cent in 2007 (see Figure 9).

Workers in the United States are now working more hours and have increased their productivity, yet their pay is declining while increasing wealth, as we have seen, is going exclusively to the economic elite.

> If our income had kept pace with compensation distribution rates established in the early 1970s, we would all be making at least three times as much as we are currently making. How different would your life be if you were making $120,000 a year, instead of $40,000? . . .
>
> What could be done with all the money that has been hoarded by the Economic Elite is extraordinary. . . . On top of what should be our average six-figure yearly income, we could have: 1) free health care

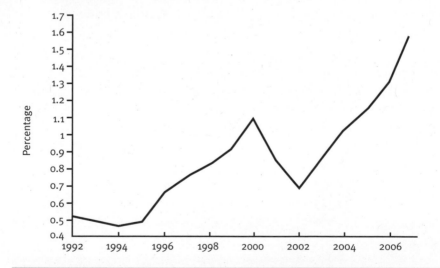

Figure 8. Percentage of total national income that went to the top 400 US families.

for every American; 2) a free four-bedroom home for every American family; 3) 5% tax rate for 99% of Americans; 4) drastically improved public education and free college for all; and 5) significantly improved public transportation and infrastructure. . . . Outside of outdated and obsolete economic models and theories there is no reason why all this money should be kept in the hands of a few, at the immense suffering and expense of the many.[8]

The mainstream media will always hide the immense individual suffering and psychological toll that lies behind this reality. The news will continue to be about numbers that show fabricated improvements for the purpose of continuing to satisfy the greed of the mega-rich.

Persistence of a failed ideology

There seems to be no doubt that 1970 was a tremendously significant turning point, affecting not only the life of Americans but of the world as a whole. But what happened in 1970? As we will see in the next chapter, the late 1960s consolidated, through the 'Big Eight' universities of the United States, the neoliberal paradigm as the definitive one, as a result of the lavish research

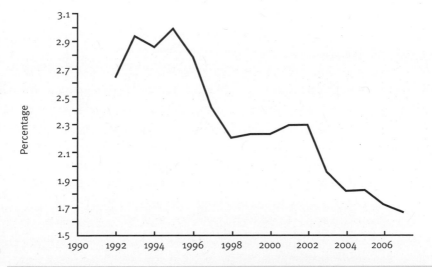

Figure 9. Effective tax rate on the top-earning 400 US families.

programme launched by the RAND Corporation and the US Air Force for the purpose of promoting advanced research in mathematical economics. In other words, 1970 became the year of the neoliberal triumph. From 1970 onwards, with the imposition of the neoliberal ideology (through Reaganism and Thatcherism in the US and UK, and later in the rest of Europe), the US Gini coefficient starts to grow while quality of life starts to decline, as shown in the first graph of Figure 3 in Chapter 10 (page 147). What is noteworthy is that the same happens in the other countries shown in the figure, as well as in many others not shown there. In all cases, the decline of quality of life begins between 1970 and 1985, depending on when each country adopted the neoliberal doctrine.

The indicators we have shown clearly reveal that neoliberalism after 40 years has not delivered what it was supposed to deliver – that is, an increase in global welfare – but rather the opposite. However, this fact does not seem to disturb mainstream economists, who still believe that improvements result from more of the same.

It is absolutely astonishing that the United States has imposed on the rest of the world as being desirable an economic ideology that has devastated its own country as well as many others. The fact that economists of that nation and its universities are capable of ignoring reality, and, despite all the evidence to the contrary, continuing to presume that what they do, advise and teach in terms of economics is adequate, is an epistemological and political monstrosity.

If mainstream economists resembled – even a little bit – the natural scientists whose equals they presume to be, they would be falling over each other to proclaim that their theories and methods are wrong, have failed and need to be urgently replaced by new ones. Nothing of the sort is happening, which confirms once again that what the mainstream dictates is not the need to understand reality, but to defend the practice that if theory doesn't fit reality, you have to forget reality, especially if this benefits the rich and the powerful.

This must come to an end! It probably will (as we stated at the end of the previous chapter) when the holders of this disastrous official truth die, and a new generation replaces them. That new generation is already waiting in the wings. Another world will soon be possible.

Chapter 12

A non-toxic teaching of economics

No significant changes in the economy can be expected unless the teaching of economics undergoes a deep transformation. Throughout this book we have shown that, on the one hand, the economic models that became dominant in different periods were always those that reinforced the status quo of an unjust society; and on the other, that in order for economics to have the authority to impose its propositions, it had to appear as a hard science. The latter was achieved through the use and abuse of mathematics, as a result of a kind of inferiority complex on the part of nineteenth-century economists because they weren't physicists. That is why it is never admitted that economic models are wrong. If they don't work, it's not because of a failure of the model but because reality plays foul tricks. 'If the theory doesn't fit reality, forget reality.' All this is, of course, the result of the way economics is taught in universities.

Now, if we want to change something, we must first understand the origins of that which we want to change. Neoliberalism, the offspring of neoclassical economics, has become the political ideology that dominates almost all economics departments in our universities. In fact it was the universities that gave rise to neoliberalism and continue enthusiastically to promote it as the only definitive and respectable school of economic thought. The evidence that, especially during 2008 and 2009, has shown the neoliberal doctrine to be not only wrong but poisonous does not seem to disturb those who still control the immense majority of economics departments.

The emergence of neoliberalism

Where does neoliberalism come from? The story begins almost a century and a half ago, in 1870, when economists made a case to demonstrate that economics was a science just as is Newtonian physics. The most important economists of that time, Stanley Jevons and Leon Walras, were simply fascinated with classical mechanics. Hence, they had to develop a model that had similar properties to the model of the universe designed by Newton.
As described by Edward Fullbrook:

> Whether or not economies and their markets have the same formal properties of Newton's model was never an issue. Jevons, like Walras a few years later, had discovered the delusional and contagious delights of upside-down science. Whereas Newton, backed by a century of *empirical research*, had identified fundamental properties of the physical universe and then modelled them, Jevons and Walras set about *defining* a set of concepts that could be combined in a manner formally analogous to the physical relations modelled by classical mechanics. It is these ego-servicing *a priori* concepts, which . . . are hammered into the heads of undergraduates as if they were scientific truths, that today underpin Neoliberalism.[1]

As we showed in Chapter 5, just as Newtonian physics proposed gravitation as a universal law describing the behaviour of the universe, neoclassical economists had to devise a similarly universal law capable of describing the behaviour of human beings. Such a universal law turned out to be 'utility', meaning that every human being always behaves and acts in such a way as to maximize his/her utility. Although utility is never clearly defined, it is essentially material and refers to that which can be measured. Having found the universal law, the next step was to adopt an adequate language for their physicalization of economics. So:

> In neoclassical economics 'bodies' translates 'individuals' or 'agents'; 'motions' translates 'exchange of goods'; 'forces', translates 'preferences' which when summed become 'supply and demand'; 'mechanical equilibrium' becomes 'market equilibrium', this being when the difference between supply and demand is zero; and 'physical systems'

translates 'markets'. But this is only the beginning of the neoclassical fabrication. To make the model determinate it was necessary to define the terms 'exchange of goods', 'individuals' and 'preferences', and thereby 'markets' in bizarre ways. All exchanges were said to magically take place at the prices that equated demand and supply. There were no disjunctions from innovation and competition and no distortions from oligopoly or monopoly. This elimination of dynamics placed the focus entirely on when the market is in equilibrium, thereby ignoring actual market processes. Individuals were defined as atomistic, that is as having no social dimension, and within their isolated selves as being one-dimensional, meaning that they have only one criteria, preference satisfaction, for making decisions. And the preferences of these non-social beings were defined as unchanging, completely independent of life experiences, including consumer ones.[2]

In his *Elements of Pure Economics* (1877) Walras sets out to demonstrate that this pure theory of economics is a science that resembles the physico-mathematical sciences in every respect. The way of demonstrating this 'every respect' was achieved through the imposition of complex, and sometimes even nonsensical, mathematical formalisms that have no relation whatsoever to real-life economics.

Neoclassical economics in today's world

It should be noted that although the fabrication of the neoclassical economists was successful, and accepted as legitimate by the academic communities, it coexisted with other visions, such as the institutional economics as proposed by Veblen and others. During the 1930s, without disappearing, it was displaced by Keynesianism, yet continued to coexist with it as well as with other approaches, such as those proposed by the Marxians. Other schools, such as the Post-Keynesianist, Austrian, Behaviourist and Feminist, added their own contributions up to the late 1960s. Up to then, students such as myself (Manfred) had the option of multiple perspectives when analysing economic problems, and courses such as Economic History and History of Economic Thought – now completely vanished from the curricula – were fundamental in every department of economics.

The extraordinary thing about nineteenth-century neoclassical economics is that it has achieved its final success in the late twentieth century. This is amazing indeed. We no longer have a physics of the nineteenth century, nor a nineteenth-century biology or astronomy or geology or engineering. All sciences have shown a permanent evolution. Economics is the only discipline where problems of the twenty-first century are supposed to be interpreted, analysed and understood using nineteenth-century theories. In a necrological impulse, 'mainstream' economists of today look for guidance and inspiration in a cemetery of 150 years ago, as if nothing had happened since. This is preposterous to say the least, and the fact that universities go along with it is, as we see it, an epistemological scandal of immense proportions.

The academic coexistence of different economic visions and schools that lasted inside the universities until the late 1960s has been totally erased. There are, of course, many economists who do not adhere to the mainstream and are producing important alternative contributions in their field. However, their work is recognized by neither economics departments nor traditional mainstream journals. Their work is subversive and has to be carried out beyond the walls of university orthodoxy. Harvard University provides an interesting example. At the time of writing (2010), introductory economics is taught by Gregory Mankiw, author of the dominant textbook in the world today. Some students have felt that his course is a 'massive conservative propaganda'. Hence, when a new similar course was proposed by Professor Marty Feldstein, ex-adviser to President Reagan, students protested. Another introductory course, with a critical and pluralist orientation, is now being taught by professor Stephen Marglin. But while Mankiw's course assigns credits to the students, Marglin's is not entitled to give such credits. What stupid fundamentalism in Harvard University, one of the greatest universities in the world!

Things being as they are, it is not surprising that economists overlooked the collapse of the economy in October 2008 – the biggest collapse since 1930. Probably not more than two or three economists in the United States predicted the crisis. One of them, Nouriel Roubini, was dismissed by colleagues as being catastrophic in outlook and criticized for not using mathematical models in his prediction.

As an epistemological event, the 2008 meltdown of the global financial system ranks with the observation of the 1919 solar eclipse.[3] If professional practice in economics resembled, even in the slightest, that in the natural sciences, then in the wake of today's global disaster economists would be falling over each other to proclaim the falsity of their theories, the inadequacy of their methods and the urgent need for new ones.[4]

Nothing of the sort is happening. Today what we still have, instead of economic education, is economic indoctrination.

The neoclassical lobby

The opportunity for neoclassical economics to slowly push other economic visions out of the way was dramatically enhanced during the late 1960s when the RAND Corporation and the United States Air Force (institutions backed by the Pentagon) launched a lavish programme to fund research in mathematical economics. The reason was that military experts believed that game theory and other mathematical tools could be important for national defence. Most of the money went to the 'Big Eight' universities – California, Harvard, Princeton, Columbia, Stanford, Chicago, Yale and M.I.T. – which happily adapted the orientation of their economics departments so as to guarantee the continuous flux of those massive financial resources. Given the weight and the international prestige of the Big Eight, the fact that they consecrated neoclassical economics as the definitive economic doctrine inevitably induced other universities of the Western world to follow suit. Furthermore, over 1,000 economists – the great majority – employed since the late 1960s by the International Monetary Fund and the World Bank have gone through the indoctrination of the Big Eight. It should therefore be no surprise that during the last three decades of the twentieth century and the beginning of the new millennium, neoliberalism, as an economic doctrine, has managed to dominate the entire world. The terrible harm that those generations of economists have done, especially to the developing world, has been amply illustrated in previous chapters.

From the perspective of a 'normal' academic mind, it is really difficult to understand how such an unreal, simplistic and dogmatic intellectual construction has managed to seduce and even to convince academia, politicians and the general public that the fantasy world from which its conclusions are drawn is actually the real world. Once again, Fullbrook illustrates this very well.

> In the neoclassical make-believe world everything, like in a fairytale, works wondrously well. There is never any unemployment, markets of all kinds always clear instantly; everyone gets exactly what they deserve; market outcomes are invariantly 'optimal'; everyone maximizes their potential; and all citizens possess a crystal ball that infallibly foresees the future. In this axiomatic paradise (without messy things like social beings, institutions, history, culture, ethics, religion, human development and the indeterminacy that always accompanies freedom) there is no government ownership, no regulation, no corporate accountability, no building codes, no health and safety laws, no collective bargaining rights, no food standards, no controls on oligopoly and monopoly, no welfare, no public health departments, etc., etc. Instead there are just 'markets'. Markets, markets, markets. For those who take the model literally, the solution to all human problems is to make the real world more like the neoclassical make-believe world. 'All you need are markets.' If you can't yet get rid of something that is not a market, then make it look like a market. That is the central idea of neoliberalism. Simpleminded? Of course. Deluded? Totally. But . . . it can be applied to virtually everything.[5]

This must come to an end, because economists trained according to these fantasies end up being like *idiot savants*: geniuses when playing with mathematical symbols but totally ignorant of the real world in which they live.

Even now (2010), after breakdowns and crises that have been the consequence of ignorance and blindness about the real world, we find economists whose argument is that we must simply design better models. They don't realize that the only way to achieve a better understanding of reality is to appreciate once again economic history and the history of economic ideas. In other words, what we need is to have cultured economists again. As suggested by Hodgson:

> To understand the current economic crisis we have to look at both economic history and the history of economic thought. To under-

stand how economics has taken a wrong turning we have to appreciate work in the philosophy of economics and the relationship between economics and ideology. These unfashionable discourses have to be brought back into the centre of the economic curricula and rehabilitated as vital areas of enquiry.[6]

Dissent in academia

To continue promoting a poisonous ideology disguised as science is suicidal. The cure is certainly not easy, but it has begun. In late 2000 a group of economics graduate students in France launched a petition accusing economics of being an "autistic science" and expressed their desire to "escape from imaginary worlds". They criticized the fact that only the neoclassical school was being taught, leaving out all other manifestations of economic thought, and claimed that mathematics had been turned into an end in itself instead of being a tool. Furthermore, they opposed dogmatism and protested about the absence of criticism and debate in the classes. Finally, they proposed the return to a pluralistic approach in the teaching of economics. The first paragraph of the petition is worth quoting.

> **We wish to escape from imaginary worlds**. Most of us have chosen to study economics so as to acquire a deep understanding of the economic phenomena with which the citizens of today are confronted. But the teaching that is offered, that is to say for the most part neoclassical theory or approaches derived from it, does not generally answer this expectation. Indeed, even when the theory legitimately detaches itself from contingencies in the first instance, it rarely carries out the necessary return to the facts. The empirical side (historical facts, functioning of institutions, study of the behaviour and strategies of the agents . . .) is almost nonexistent. Furthermore, this gap in the teaching, this disregard for concrete realities, poses an enormous problem for those who would like to render themselves useful to economic and social actors.[7]

One month after the students' petition was launched, a second petition , this time signed by a number of economics professors, saw the light. The professors did not only agree with the statements of the students, but they identified the five problems that should be overcome in the teaching of economics: 1) The exclusion of theory that is not neoclassical from the curriculum; 2) The mismatch between economics teaching and economic reality; 3) The use of mathematics as an end in itself rather than as a tool; 4) Teaching methods that exclude or prohibit critical thinking; 5) The need for a plurality of approaches adapted to the complexity of objects analysed. Their first paragraph is also worth quoting.

> In real sciences, explanation is focused on actual phenomena. The validity and relevancy of a theory can only be assessed through a confrontation with 'facts'. This is why we, along with many students, deplore the development of a pedagogy in economics privileging the presentation of theories and the building and manipulation of models without considering their empirical relevance. This pedagogy highlights the formal properties of model construction, while largely ignoring the relations of models, if any, to economic realities. This is scientism. Under a scientific approach, on the other hand, the first interest is to demonstrate the informative power and efficiency of an abstraction *vis-à-vis* sets of empirical phenomena. This should be the primary task of the economist. It is not a mathematical issue.[8]

The impact extended to other countries. A few months later, PhD students at the University of Cambridge published their own petition, and a year later economists from 17 countries gathered in Kansas City, USA, released their International Open Letter to all departments of economics calling on them to reform economics education and research. They called for: 1) A broader conception of human behaviour; 2) Recognition of culture; 3) Consideration of history; 4) A new theory of knowledge; 5) Empirical grounding; 6) Expanded methods; and 7) Interdisciplinary dialogue. In March 2003 economics students at Harvard launched their own petition, demanding a new introductory course that would have "better balance and coverage of a broader spectrum of views" and that would "not only teach students the accepted modes of thinking, but also challenge students to think critically and deeply about conventional truths". The course is now being taught in Harvard, but we mentioned earlier in this chapter what happened with it. While the 'mainstream' course taught by Mankiw gives credits to students, the new course taught by Marglin does not.

A growing number of students and academics from other universities, including those in Hispanic countries, have been and continue joining the movement. However, economics departments in the immense majority of universities remain unaffected.

What we have now are two parallel worlds. One 'mainstream', still anchored in the economics departments, immune to all messages and evidence that might bring about any change; and the 'alternatives', dispersed all over the place and perceived by the 'mainstream' as subversive agents, but still incapable of bringing about the fall of the neoliberal wall. Sooner or later, however, the wall will collapse. We are in the situation so lucidly described by the great Max Planck over 100 years ago, when he was faced with the orthodoxy of the Maxwellian physicists: "A new scientific truth does not triumph by convincing its opponents and making them see the light, but rather because its opponents eventually die, and a new generation grows up that is familiar with it."

The situation in which we are now is precisely that of a growing new generation waiting to attend the funeral of the 'official' holders of the truth.

And now, why not indulge in a little Aristotelian dream? Let us imagine that economics becomes again the manner of managing the household in order to achieve *the art of living and living well,* respecting the right of all others to achieve the same, within the limits of the carrying capacity of our planet.

Chapter 13

Implementation: from the village to a global order

When introducing in public the alternative paradigm for a more humane economy, as described in the previous chapter, people often ask how it would work in practice or how such principles could be articulated into policy. In other words, the concern is about implementation, but in fact such policies are already being implemented in hundreds of places. The point is that policy is generally perceived as a macro top-down process that makes the news, and not as a bottom-up grassroots phenomenon that remains hidden in the consciousness of those directly involved in the actions, and very rarely appears in the media.

What is described in this chapter is essentially a process that involves many projects. Converging around common principles, orientations and values, these projects together build an alternative paradigm of development that goes upwards, from the village to a global order.[1] Despite the fact that the number of cases is enormous, they are generally perceived as being of no more than anecdotal interest. Paul Hawken describes the situation clearly.

> Movements . . . have followers. This movement, however, doesn't fit the standard model. It is dispersed, inchoate, and fiercely independent. It has no manifesto or doctrine, no overriding authority to check with. It is taking shape in schoolrooms, farms, jungles, villages, companies, deserts, fisheries, slums – and yes, even fancy New York hotels. One of its distinctive features is that it is tentatively emerging as a global humanitarian movement arising from the bottom up. Historically, social movements have arisen primarily in response to injustice, inequities and corruption. Those woes still remain legion,

joined by a new condition that has no precedent: the planet has a life-threatening disease, marked by massive ecological degradation and rapid climate change. As I counted the vast number of organizations it crossed my mind that perhaps I was witnessing the growth of something organic, if not biologic.

Many outside the movement critique it as powerless, but the assessment does not stop its growth. When describing it to politicians, academics, and business people, I found that many believe they are already familiar with this movement, how it works, what it consists of, and its approximate size . . . For them and others the movement is small, known and circumscribed, a new type of charity, with a sprinkling of ragtag activists who occasionally give it a bad name. People inside the movement can also underestimate it, basing their judgment on only the organizations they are linked to, even though their networks can only encompass a fraction of the whole. But after spending years researching this phenomenon, including creating with my colleagues a global database of its constituent organizations, I have come to these conclusions: *this is the largest social movement in all of human history. No one knows its scope, and how it functions is more mysterious than what meets the eye.* [Our italics]

What *does* meet the eye is compelling: coherent, organic, self-organized congregations involving tens of millions of people dedicated to change. When asked at colleges if I am pessimistic or optimistic about the future, my answer is always the same: if you look at the science that describes what is happening on Earth today and aren't pessimistic, you don't have the correct data. If you meet the people in this unnamed movement and aren't optimistic, you haven't got a heart. What I see are ordinary and some not-so-ordinary individuals willing to confront despair, power and incalculable odds in an attempt to restore some semblance of grace, justice, and beauty to this world.[2]

From power and greed to equity and respect

What we have is two parallel worlds. One concerned with politics, competition, greed and power, which seems to have everything under its control; and another concerned with equity, well-being, respect for life and solidarity, which doesn't control anything, but grows and expands as an unstoppable underground movement of civil society. The former, despite its overwhelming power and presence is, because of its rigidity, dogmatism and growth fetishism,[3] vulnerable and unsustainable, as shown by its ever-deeper crises; while the latter, because of its dispersion, its diversity, its fierce independence and its chaotic structure, cannot be beheaded nor can it collapse.

The existence of these parallel worlds reveals that we are moving, or at least intending to move, from a world of power and individualism to one of solidarity and community. Responses are emerging everywhere to environmental disasters and all forms of human suffering. The need for a radical change of the dominant economic model underlies all the components of the movement.

Despite the vigour with which this immense underground grows, one often hears comments to the effect that environmentalism, and more generally a new economics, have failed as a movement and are dead. In fact, the opposite is true. Sooner or later everyone will be an environmentalist as a consequence of necessity and experience. The belief that problems can be solved individually, from the top down is, at this stage, clearly out of the question. "The world is a system, and it will soon be a very different world, driven by millions of communities who believe that democracy and restoration are grassroots movements that connect us to values that we hold in common".[4]

The initiatives for change that emerge from civil society are similar to the immune system of a living being. You don't see it, you don't feel it, but it is there working in order to protect the body to which it belongs. The body feels the disease, which is the enemy, but does not feel the underground army that attacks the disease. We are aware of deep crises and profound problems affecting our lives and, as a consequence, often feel depressed and defeated. But we should also be aware of the fact that if our immune system did not exist, things would be much worse. It is impossible to estimate how many infections and wounds that could harm our social body are avoided every minute and everywhere due to the actions of those invisible millions of the underground network of civil society.

In his Natural Capital Institute in California, Paul Hawken and his colleagues have created an immense database of civil society organizations in 243 countries, territories and regions, which amount to close to 300,000. This is, of course, only a fraction of all the groups that exist worldwide. The classification scheme that emerged from the mapping of the landscape covers literally thousands of disciplines and concerns. The main headings (under each one of which are many subcategories) are: Agriculture and Farming, Air, Biodiversity, Business and Economics, Children and Youth, Coastal Ecosystems, Community Development, Cultural Heritage, Democracy, Ecology, Education, Energy, Fisheries, Forestry, Climate Change, Globalization, Governance, Greening of Industry, Health, Human Rights, Indigenous People, Inland Water Ecosystems, Media, Mining, Plants, Pollution, Population, Poverty Eradication, Property Rights, Seniors, Sustainability, Sustainable Cities, Sustainable Development, Technology, Terrestrial Ecosystems, Water, Wildlife, Women and Work.[5]

Such an enormous network of civil society initiatives is a colossal immune system that, once the global top-down power system reaches its final crisis, will be capable of giving rise to a new bottom-up democracy, based on solidarity and cooperation, that will expand from the village to a global order and offer the answers for the construction of a more humane world.

The following are some concrete examples of the concerns and actions of civil groups that relate to our proposed new economy – examples that are coherent with the five principles for a twenty-first-century economics outlined in Chapter 10. We start with a short history of Human Scale Development, and continue with experiences in Colombia and Sweden – two very different contexts yet with similar aims.

Human Scale Development

During the early 1980s the Dag Hammarskjöld Foundation of Sweden launched a programme under the name of 'From the Village to a Global Order'. Part of that programme was the research team of the Development Alternatives Centre (CEPAUR) that I (Manfred) headed and whose purpose was to propose an alternative economics. In 1986, after three years of work and discussions in several international seminars that convened academics and experts with similar interests, CEPAUR generated a document outlining the principles of Human Scale Development and its Theory of Fundamental Human Needs. The final text was published by the Foundation, firstly in Spanish and two years later in English. Through the Foundation's network the text was distributed in most Latin American countries. It generated an almost immediate interest and enthusiasm, not only among dissident academics and alternative groups but also, to our great surprise, among many peasant and Indian communities in South America. We were absolutely astonished when we realized that the original Spanish version became in those days the most photocopied document on the continent. We used to arrive in Andean communities to be approached by local leaders with a photocopy of a photocopy of a photocopy, almost unreadable, ready to discuss whether their interpretation was correct and whether their projects satisfied the philosophy of Human Scale Development. It was moving to witness how such marginal communities adopted the principles and designed local development projects that conventional experts would have been unable to conceive. Many of those projects have survived and flourished. One of them, the Peasant Development Association, is described later in this chapter.

The first lesson we learned from those experiences was that the language of Human Scale Development and its Needs Theory can be easily understood by simple people who lack any formal education beyond a few years of primary school. The second lesson was that no true development can succeed without the understanding, participation and creativity of the people themselves. The third lesson was that what mobilizes common people does not necessarily mobilize academics. In fact, what took the peasants almost no time to understand took about 15 years to generate interest at academic levels. Now Human Scale Development is finally in the academic system, and its Human Needs Theory is recognized as one of the most important contributions in the field.[6]

Human needs, quality of life and well-being are what people understand – not the abstractions of macroeconomic indicators that have nothing to do with real life. Development is about people, not about objects. The fact that once again civil society is willing to rediscover and respect human feelings and the value of all manifestations of life means that a better world is possible, even if it is not mentioned in the news delivered by the power-controlled media.

The Peasant Development Association

La Cocha is a lake located in Colombia's Southern Department of Nariño, close to the border with Ecuador. It is surrounded by a large number of small farmer and peasant holdings. Traditionally the main economic activity was the exploitation of the forests in order to use the timber for the production of charcoal. During the late 1980s, when a group of farmers had become aware of the principles of Human Scale Development and realized that deforestation was beginning to have devastating effects, an initiative was undertaken to organize the community around alternative forms of income generation. This led to the constitution in 1991 of an association named Minga Asoyarcocha,[7] which declared all its holdings as Private Natural Reserves of Civil Society – a concept unknown at the time in Colombia. As a result, 4,000 hectares became protected land, including wetlands, temperate rainforest and biodiversity, generating what were then identified as biological corridors.

From the very beginning the Minga organized educational programmes promoting social, economic, political and cultural principles based on the respect for all forms of life, the sustainable use of biodiversity, and human-scale development for all members of the community. All holdings were divided according to zones that facilitated the best alternatives for soil use, prioritizing food security and greater levels of self-reliance. The reserves became spaces for interdisciplinary work and research about biodiversity, ecology, agroecology and sustainability in the use of natural resources. Politically the Minga is based on a direct democracy, with full participation of all members of the community. This has allowed the strengthening of their power as a civil society to such a degree that they have been able to stop the construction of two megaprojects that would have dramatically altered the whole region.

Family income of the members of the Minga has increased to 2.77 times above the regional average, and 1.8 times above the national average. In terms of self-reliance, traditionally they produced around 40 per cent of the food consumed, and now they produce 83 per cent. The use of chemicals has been totally eliminated, so all agricultural production is organic. All families of the community leave 66 per cent of their holdings for conservation, compared with not more than 20 per cent conserved by non-members. The initiatives of reforestation and regeneration that the Minga has undertaken have facilitated again the movement of migratory birds, which can be observed as a result of the increase in the number and variety of species. This has generated an enormous interest among members of the community, so that now it is common to find adults and children who record the taxonomy, the feeding habits and the migratory routes of the majority of birds that appear in the region.

The Minga Asoyarcocha has had both regional and national impacts. In the department of Nariño, three additional Mingas have been created, following the same principles, and by joining together have given rise to the Peasant Development Association (ADC).[8] The success of this structure is due to the fact that all productive projects, as well as other initiatives, are designed in coherence with the ecological, geographical and cultural characteristics of the different areas. This is promoted through the voluntary work of different active groups, such as the Network of Natural Reserves, the Soil Recoverers, the Community Communicators, Women in Action, the Agroecological Producers and the Sociocultural Group. At the national level the ADC became the co-founder of the Colombian Network of Natural Reserves of Civil Society, which promotes similar initiatives in other regions of the country.

The concept of sustainability of the ADC is mainly based on intergenerational concerns. This has resulted in what is probably its most beautiful initiative: the Programme of the Inheritors of the Planet, the purpose of which is to create spaces for children and youth in order to give them the opportunity to develop their artistic, cultural, crafts, environmental and playing abilities and capacities, allowing them to take ethically based decisions and become true creators of their own lives. At the time of writing the programme includes 512 children and teenagers linked to five different groups, called the Friends of Nature, the Toucans, the Orchid, Gualmaventura and Green Life.

The ADC must assure the continuity of the organization and its philosophy of community, solidarity and cooperation. A relief generation of 18 young members is already studying at university those disciplines that will allow them to contribute as advisors in order to bring about better leadership, administration and technical efficiency of the Mingas and the ADC. Before going into formal higher education, children and teenagers go through a centre that gives them guidance on how to become capable of generating an attractive and familial social and political context that ensures the tenure of the peasants in their territory and allows for the development of a production model that is environmentally sane, economically viable, socially just and culturally acceptable.

A fundamental principle promoted by the community is what they call the "dialogue of knowledge", as a recognition of the importance of traditional cultural, spiritual and organizational values of the peasants that have been discredited by modern techniques and attitudes. Through this they make a continuing effort to recover and honour ancestral wisdoms.

The ADC has become an outstanding example of successful bottom-up sustainable development, promoting self-reliance, a spirit of community and harmony with nature. In 2007 its project 'Cultivating the diversity of the Colombian Southeast, an alternative of conservation and well-being according to the principles of human scale development' was awarded the national environmental prize, the Blue Planet Prize.

In its effort to promote dialogue and share experiences, since the 1990s the ADC has organized three international seminars: in 1996 with 200 participants from 14 countries, in 1998 with 280 participants from 11 countries, and in 2010 with 250 participants from mainly Latin American countries. The seminars consist of sharing dreams about the future. In fact the participants identify themselves as 'dream designers', and all the presentations and papers must consist of designed dreams. In the sessions and round tables it is interesting to see peasants discussing as equals with politicians, academics and experts; often the interventions of the peasants are the most creative and substantial. The seminars go on for five days, and include not only discussions but also excursions, exhibitions of crafts, folklore, music, poetry and other cultural expressions.

What is especially fascinating is that while the seminar takes place on one side of the lake, on the opposite side another seminar, with the same topics and questions, is run by the Inheritors of the Planet. At the end of the first day a delegation of four members of the main seminar crosses the lake in order to inform the children about the results of their meeting. At the end of the second day a delegation of the children crosses the lake in order to inform the adults about their discussions and conclusions. The same happens on the following two days. The culmination occurs with a joint final meeting on the fifth day, which becomes an unforgettably enriching experience for the participants.

Emulation of the ADC example is taking place in many rural areas of Latin America. Having worked for the FAO (Food and Agriculture Organization) and ILO (International Labour Organization) as a development expert in the field, I (Manfred) never found a development project organized by official institutions as successful as those that originated as bottom-up self-reliant community initiatives. The case of ADC is in my experience the most conspicuous example, but there are many more all over the world. Why don't they make the news? According to my experience, the answer is that for the development bureaucracy a conventional failure is more acceptable than an unconventional success.

Eco-municipalities

In the mid 1980s a little town of 6,000 inhabitants in northern Sweden called Övertornea received the national prize of Municipality of the Year. Its history confirms the strengths of the bottom-up process in the sense that a local initiative, no matter how small, can have great and significant impacts – very often even greater and more significant than the top-down approaches practised by large-scale politics. The main speaker in the award ceremony compared the town to a bumblebee. He reminded his listeners of Igor Sikorsky, a famous aeronautical engineer of the early twentieth century, who hung in his office lobby a sign that read: "The bumblebee, according to the calculations of our engineers, cannot fly at all, but the bumblebee doesn't know this and flies."

Övertornea was hit very hard by the 1980 economic recession, which raised unemployment to 20 per cent, losing as a consequence 25 per cent of its population compared with 30 years earlier. Many experts predicted that the region was doomed to die. No solution seemed to exist, and people were affected by apathy and a lack of mutual trust. It was then that the municipal government decided to explore other possibilities for the future.

Together with members of the community, the municipal government made a commitment to create a process of development that was in harmony with nature. It had to be a win-win-win relationship between humans, society and nature. Residents began to realize that investing with an ecological orientation would bring about economically positive effects. To characterize the transformation they were initiating, Övertornea began to call itself an 'eco-municipality'. As related by Torbjörn Lahti:

> Övertornea was discussing and practising ideas such as mobilizing people, taking a bottom-up approach to community planning, collaborative community development, cooperating across department and industrial sector boundaries, investing in local culture, and taking into account the local informal economy. Such ideas were foreign to conventional Swedish town planning and community development practices at that time. What the regional and national establishments could see, without understanding why, was that these strange ideas evidently produced remarkable results.

> Key to these successes was widespread community participation. The citizens of Övertornea took on the community development work to become the town they wanted. In the six years following this decision, 200 new companies in Övertornea developed and prospered. These new enterprises included organic farms, beekeeping, fish farms, cheap husbandry and eco-tourism enterprises. Over 600 residents took part in special study circles discussing regional development issues and future possibilities. Out of these study circles emerged village development associations that took charge of the ideas sprouting and gradually taking form. The ecological perspective blossomed in a municipal government investment in biofuelled district heating, support for ecological farming such as farmer education and municipal purchasing of organic foods, establishing a 'health home' and building an ecovillage to attract new families.[9]

As proof that there is nothing so small that it cannot produce large and unexpected effects (like the moving wings of a butterfly in China producing a hurricane in the Caribbean), the news of Övertornea's transformation spread through the country over the next few years. Inspired in part by its revitalization as a small town, a national movement of 3,300 similar village development groups evolved, where hundreds of thousands of village inhabitants began to take part in developing their communities in the direction that they wanted.

During the early 1990s similar eco-community developments were started in Norway, Denmark and Finland. Collaboration among these Nordic eco-cities and eco-towns brought about a combined Nordic eco-community presentation at the 1992 United Nations Rio Summit on Sustainable Development. Much of the Agenda 21 produced by the Summit in relation to local sustainable development emerged from the Nordic contribution. Thus the United Nations' world guide to local sustainable development urges communities to begin to work in the same manner in which Övertornea had begun to work ten years earlier. Again, this is an example of where the work of a single cell of the planet's immune system makes the invisible visible. And it is the visible, of course, that makes the news.

The whole process described here has given rise to institutions that are also important elements for the survival, the strengthening and the diffusion of the process. Some give it scientific backing and orientation; others education and assistance.

The Natural Step Framework

The foundations come from The Natural Step Framework's four Conditions for Sustainability or 'System Conditions'. The following description of the Natural Step Framework is given on the Alliance for Sustainability website.[10]

The scientific consensus principles on which the Natural Step Framework (NSF) is based were used by Swedish physicist Dr John Holmberg and Natural Step (NS) founder and Swedish medical doctor and oncologist Dr Karl-Henrik Robèrt to generate four basic 'system conditions' or conditions of sustainability, which are the focus of the NSF and have been modified as stated below.

The Natural Step Framework holds that in a sustainable society, nature won't be subject to:
1. systematically increasing concentrations of substances extracted from the Earth's crust
2. systematically increasing concentration of substances produced by society
3. degradation by physical means.

And in that society:
4. human needs are met worldwide.

To address the first three, strategies include both dematerialization (using fewer resources to accomplish the same task), substitution of alternatives, more efficient use of materials and the 'three Rs': Reduce, Reuse, Recycle, in addition to composting. Here is an easy-to-understand, practical way of addressing the principles:

1. What we take from the Earth: mining and fossil fuels. Avoid systematically increasing concentrations of substances extracted from the Earth's crust. Simply stated, we need to use renewable energy and non-toxic, reusable materials to avoid the spread of hazardous mined metals and pollutants. Why? Mining and burning fossil fuels release a wide range of substances that do not go away, but rather continue to build up and spread in the ecosphere. Nature has adapted over millions of years to specific amounts of materials. Cells don't know how to handle significant amounts of lead, mercury, radioactive materials and other hazardous compounds from mining; this often leads to learning disabilities, the weakening of immune systems and birth defects. The burning of fossil fuels generates dangerous levels of pollutants, contributing to smog, acid rain and global climate change.

We can support policies that take action to reduce our overall energy use. We can drive less, use car pools, use public transportation, ride bicycles or walk. We can conserve energy through energy-efficient lighting, proper insulation, passive solar technologies, and reduced heating and cooling. We can support a shift to renewable energy such as solar and wind power instead of nuclear, coal or petroleum. We can also decrease our use of mined metals and minerals through recycling, reuse and preferably reduced consumption. We can avoid chemical fertilizers.

2. What we make: chemicals, plastics and other substances. Nature must not be subject to systematically increasing concentrations of substances produced by society. Simply stated, we need to use safe, biodegradable substances that do not cause the spread of toxins in the environment. Why? Since the Second World War our society has produced more than 85,000 chemicals such as DDT and PCBs. Many of these substances, which are unknown to nature, do not go away but rather spread and bio-accumulate in nature and in the fat cells of animals and humans. Cells don't know how to handle significant amounts of these chemicals, often leading to cancer, hormone disruption, improper development, birth defects and long-term genetic change.

We can support green procurement policies and use non-toxic natural cleaning materials and personal care products. We can decrease our use of plastics and reuse the ones we have, such as plastic bags, plates, cups and eating utensils. We can stop using CFCs and other ozone-depleting substances. We can use safe, natural pest control in our schools, parks, homes, lawns and gardens. We can support farmers in becoming sustainable and eliminating hazardous pesticides by using our money to buy certified organic food and clothing. We can support the elimination of factory farming and slurry ponds that cause air and water pollution.

3. What we do to the Earth: biodiversity and ecosystems. Nature must not be subject to degradation by physical means. Simply stated, we need to protect our soils, water and air, or we won't be able to eat, drink or breathe. Why? Forests, soils, wetlands, lakes, oceans and other naturally productive ecosystems provide food, fibres, habitat, oxygen, waste handling, temperature moderation and a host of essential goods and services. For millions of years they have been purifying the planet and creating a habitat suitable for human and other life. When we destroy or deplete these systems, we endanger both our livelihoods and the future of human existence.

We can purchase certified, sustainably harvested forest products rather than destroying rainforests. We can reduce or eliminate our consumption of products that are not sustainably harvested, such as certain types of fish and seafood. We can shop with reusable bags rather than using more paper and plastic bags. We can decrease our use of water and use composting toilets that return valuable nutrients to the Earth. We can fight urban sprawl and encourage the cleaning up of brownfield and other contaminated sites. We can support smart growth and safeguard endangered species by protecting wildlife habitats.

4. Meeting fundamental human needs. Human needs are to be met worldwide. Simply stated, we can use less stuff and save money while meeting the needs of every human on this planet. Why? The US makes up only 4 per cent of the world's population but consumes over 25 per cent of its resources. The lowest 20 per cent of earners receive only 1.4 per cent of the world's income. In order to survive they can see no alternative to cutting down rainforests, selling endangered species and using polluting energy sources.

We need to make business, government and non-profit-making organizations aware that we can achieve the ten-fold increase in efficiency needed to become sustainable, and in some cases, a hundred-fold increase in productivity that will save money, create jobs and reduce waste as part of a new Industrial Revolution. We can encourage discussion about fundamental needs, as proposed by Manfred Max-Neef in his Theory of Human Scale Development.[11] We can ask if we really need more stuff, and design our workplaces, homes and organizations to give us less of what we don't want (pollution, stress and expense) and more of what we want (healthy, attractive and nurturing environments) and, above all, a sense of community between ourselves and all forms of life.

The Institute for Eco-Municipality Education and Assistance

The educational component of the process has been established by the Institute for Eco-Municipality Education and Assistance. The information that follows has been taken from a leaflet of the Institute.

The purpose of the Institute is to provide support for emerging eco-municipalities and those communities interested in a systematic, comprehensive approach for changing to sustainable practices. An eco-municipality is defined as a local government – a municipal or county government – that has officially adopted a particular set of sustainability principles and has committed to a bottom-up, participatory approach for implementing them. As mentioned earlier, the first eco-municipalities developed in northern Sweden in the early 1980s. Their work became the model for Agenda 21 in the 1992 Rio Summit on Sustainable Development.

The process has expanded dramatically during the last two decades. At this stage (2010) there are over 70 eco-municipalities in Sweden – almost one-third of all municipalities in the country, with Stockholm being the most important one. The movement has spread widely. In the United States several cities, towns and county governments have officially declared themselves to be eco-municipalities, adopting the same sustainability principles of their Swedish counterparts and working to systematically change their local government and larger community to sustainable practices. Similar initiatives are taking place in Kenya, Ghana, Japan, Canada and Mexico, and will soon be happening in Chile.

The role of the Institute in this expanding process is to provide education and training in how to become an eco-municipality, to develop leadership skills and municipal staff training in sustainability principles and how to change to sustainable practices – and more.

The services include workshops and presentations on:
- The eco-municipality systems approach to sustainable community change.
- The Natural Step Framework, a science-based system approach to sustainable development.
- A 'bottom-up' participatory approach to sustainable community and municipal change.

Municipal training includes:
- A science-based understanding of sustainability and its practical everyday application.
- How to translate sustainability principles into concrete, systematic change in municipal practices.
- How to integrate and institutionalize change toward sustainable practices in departmental and agency operations, policy and regulations.
- 'Train the trainer' sessions.

Community education, planning and strategy development includes:
- Bringing about broad-based community participation.
- Involving businesses and institutions.
- Sustainability education using clear principles to design action.

Eco-municipality process leadership, including:
- Advice and assistance to local governments and community organizations interested in a systematic approach to sustainable community change.
- How to design and carry out multi-year systemic change process.
- 'Process leadership' and guidance during a multi-year change process.
- Educational and training events.

Training is also given to NGOs on request.

Final reflections

It is a cause for optimism to realize that there is nothing so small and so weak that it cannot provoke an enormous and massive positive change; and that there is nothing so big and strong that it cannot dramatically collapse. Just think of the beautiful positive explosion provoked by the little community of Övertornea, located in one of the remotest places of the Earth, and compare it with the ugly and catastrophic implosion of a giant such as Lehman Brothers, located in New York. Of course, in the case of the latter the media all over the world were reporting about the massive damage to the economy and the resulting global financial disaster. Nothing has ever been reported about the healing processes that have been emerging and expanding from the bottom up, in the case of the former.

Probably the best that can happen to those of us who believe in community, in respect for all forms of life and in a more humane economy, is to remain as invisible as possible as long as the fight goes on. Invisibility, while fighting, may be after all our greatest strength. If we reach victory at the end of the day, visibility may be welcomed again.

As I am writing this chapter, in June 2010, I have just received the news that the proposal to once again legalize the killing of whales went down in flames in an international meeting in Morocco. This was mainly due to the fact that in a few weeks 1.2 million signatures from citizens all over the world were collected, amounting to the biggest whale-saving petition in history. The impact of this campaign was demonstrated by the Australian Environment Minister Peter Garret when he received the petition: "Thank you very much Avaaz.[12] It is a great pleasure to be here and accept this petition. . . . I believe the people of the world's voices need to be heard. I certainly hear them today."

Here again we have our wonderful planetary immune system doing its job.

We end with a final note of advice to those who always want to know how to implement good ideas: make an effort and try to discover what is beyond what you see. There is always much more happening if you awaken all your senses. We may still discover that a better world is possible.

References and notes

Chapter 1

1 Jeremy Naydler (2000). *Goethe on Science*, Floris Books, Edinburgh, p.23.
2 Jordi Pigem (1993). *La Odisea de Occidente*, Editorial Kairós, Barcelona.
3 Mentioned by Jeremy Naydler in *Goethe on Science*, op. cit, pp.92-3.

Chapter 2

1 I use *bourgeoisie* in the original sense (*les bourgeois*) of those whose wealth gave
   them the power to control the economic life of the community, and not in the
   sense used in the United States of *petite bourgeoisie*.
2 In the translation of George Bull (Penguin, 1961, 1975) this division is described as
   "the people and the *nobles*". In the original, Machiavelli uses *grandi*, which we
   believe is better translated as the *powerful*, referring in a democratic society to
   financial power, i.e. wealth, since in modern society wealth, not 'high' birth,
   bestows power on the possessor.
3 As an aside, we suggest that this sympathy may have been more responsible for
   the violent condemnation of Machiavelli by moralists than were his astute recommendations to rulers about how to manage their countries – recommendations the
   gist of which are followed right up to today by any self-respecting *realpolitiker*.
4 Aristotle. *Politics*, 1967, Clarendon Press, Oxford.
5 Ivonne Cruz et al. (2009). 'Towards a systemic development approach'. *Ecological
   Economics*, **68**(7), pp.2021-30.
6 It is not the intention in this chapter to recount the intellectual development of
   economic theory, but only to examine its primary societal function: the justification of the status quo. We return later to its further evolution when *utility* took the
   place of *natural law*.
7 John Maynard Keynes [1936]. *General Theory of Employment, Interest and Money*.
   Great Books, Vol. 57, third printing, 1992, Encyclopaedia Britannica and University of Chicago, p.280.
8 Adam Smith [1776]. *The Wealth of Nations*. p.170. Great Books, Vol. 36, third printing, 1992, Encyclopaedia Britannica and University of Chicago, p.33.
9 Yves Gingras (2007). 'Beautiful Mind, Ugly Deception: the Bank of Sweden Prize
   in Economics'. In Edward Fullbrook (ed.) *Real World Economics*, Anthem Press,
   London.
10 Edward Fullbrook (2009). 'Toxic Textbooks'. In Jack Reardon (ed.) *The Handbook
   of Pluralist Economics Education*, Routledge, London and New York.

Chapter 3

1 F. A. Hayek (1944). *The Road to Serfdom*. University of Chicago Press, 50th anniversary edn 1994. In the fol references the page numbers are given for the first and anniversary printings, respectively: (p.xxx/p.yyy).
2 He would have much preferred to have aimed his arrows at the Soviet Union, but Stalin was a wartime ally, and therefore untouchable.
3 Hayek, op. cit. Chapter 13, 'Totalitarians in Our Midst', p.199/p.218.
4 R. Cockett (1994). *Thinking the Unthinkable*, HarperCollins, Glasgow, pp.113-14.
5 P. Ormerod (1994). *The Death of Economics*, Faber and Faber, London, pp.115ff.
6 D. C. Coyle (1935). 'The Twilight of National Planning'. *Harper's Magazine*, October 1935, p.558.
7 Hayek, op. cit. Chapter 9, 'Security and Freedom', p.125/p.139.
8 Hayek, op. cit. Chapter 13, 'Totalitarians in our Midst', p.189/p.207.
9 John Kenneth Galbraith (1993). *The Culture of Contentment*, Penguin, Harmondsworth, p.80.
10 Cockett, op. cit. Chapter 2, p.61.
11 Clinton's press secretary, Joe Lockhart, answered reporters' questions about the reunion of the largest chunks of the Standard Oil empire by explaining that President Clinton "believes that mergers that make us more globally competitive have a positive role to play". Note that, in principle, the judiciary is independent, even in the United States.
12 A. Etzioni (1988). *The Moral Dimension*, The Free Press, New York, p.182.
13 i.e. 1981-1990.
14 William Pfaff (1993). 'When Global Competition Means Regression at Home'. *International Herald Tribune*, February 18, 1993, p.4.
15 Ibid.
16 Quoted by Samuel Brittan, 'The Myth of European "Competitiveness"'. *Financial Times*, July 1, 1993.
17 Ibid.
18 The Group of Lisbon (1995). *Limits to Competition*, The M.I.T. Press, Cambridge, Massachusetts.
19 Thomas Friedman (1993). *The Lexus and the Olive Tree*, HarperCollins, London, pp.115, 142.
20 Thomas Frank (2000). *One Market Under God*, Random House, New York, pp.93-4.
21 Lester Thurow (1999). *Building Wealth*, HarperCollins, New York, p.202.
22 Frank, op. cit., pp.96-7.

Chapter 4

1 Gunnar Myrdal (1944). *An American Dilemma, The Negro Problem and Modern Democracy*, 1962, Harper & Row, New York. The page numbers referred to in the following references are from the second (1962, one volume) edition.

2 Gunnar Myrdal (1954). *The Political Element in the Development of Economic Theory*, Harvard University Press. This book was originally published in 1930 in Swedish. It was to be almost a quarter of a century before an acceptable (to Myrdal himself) translation into English by Paul Streeten appeared.

3 Gunnar Myrdal (1969). *Objectivity in Social Research*, Pantheon Books, New York. However, the aforementioned appendix to *An American Dilemma*, 'Methods of Mitigating Biases in the Social Sciences', illustrates Myrdal's views of the subject so well that I have quoted henceforth from that appendix in preference to the later book.

4 Myrdal, *An American Dilemma*, op. cit. Appendix 2, p.1041.

5 Ibid., p.1043.

6 Ibid., p.1043.

7 Ibid., p.1044.

8 Ibid., p.1045.

9 Imagine physicists carrying out long debates as to whether the speed of light is measurable without ever lifting a hand to measure it.

10 Even Max Planck, one of the greatest 'hard scientists' in history, was prey to the fear of being judged to be irrational. He demonstrated in 1900 that the amount of electromagnetic energy (light) radiated by a body could be explained only on the basis of the assumption that light is not a continuous wave motion but manifests itself in separate bundles (quanta) of energy. But he was afraid of appearing irrational or mystical, and denied for many years that he had discovered a new, totally astounding, truth. Even thirteen years later, eight years after Albert Einstein had demonstrated that Planck's quantum hypothesis was essential to explain the photo-electric effect, Planck spoke of Einstein's acceptance of the quantum hypothesis, in his introductory presentation of Einstein to the Academy of Science in Berlin, as an unfortunate aberration of an otherwise brilliant scientist. The conviction that scientific activity is (or should be) entirely divorced from emotion is so ingrained that there are very few who would admit that fear and courage are elements in scientific work.

11 The word 'racism' is used here in its commonplace sense. There is, in fact, only one human race.

12 From the opening address at the 20th World Conference of the Society for International Development, 6 May 1991.

Chapter 5

1 Correspondence between Harrod and Robbins, 1937. See http://economia.unipv.it/harrod/edition/editionstuff/rfh.2a1.htm.

Chapter 6

1 J. L. Simon (1995). 'The State of Humanity: Steadily Improving', CATO Policy Report, **17**(5) (Sept-Oct 1995), p.131. Cato Institute, Washington DC. This quote is taken from A. A. Bartlett (2004), 'Thoughts on Long-Term Energy Supplies: Scientists and the Silent Lie', *Physics Today*, **57**(7), pp.53-5.

2   J. L. Simon (1981). *The Ultimate Resource*, Princeton University Press, p.47. Note the use of *similarly* and *because*.

3   For a number of interesting examples see Herman E. Daly and John B. Cobb (1990), *For the Common Good*, The Merlin Press, London, pp.35-41.

4   From an interview with Lomborg by Spencer Reiss. See: http://www.wired.com/wired/archive/12.06/lomborg.html.

5   Lomborg (2004), 'Need for Economists to Set Global Priorities'. Letter in *Nature*, **431** (2 September 2004), p.17. There it is stated that two-thirds of all 'climate economists', whatever that may be, are against adherence to the Kyoto Protocol.

6   For a more extensive discussion of the ideas of this remarkable thinker, see: www.hubbertpeak.com/hubbert/monetary.htm.

7   See, for example, Richard Douthwaite (1992), *The Growth Illusion*, Council Oak Books, Tulsa, Oklahoma, and Clive Hamilton (2003), *Growth Fetish*, Allen and Unwin, Sydney, Australia.

8   This phrase is taken from the subtitle of a series of two lectures entitled *Cartesian Economics*, delivered to the Student Unions of Birkbeck College and the London School of Economics on 10 and 17 November, 1921.

9   Frederick Soddy (1943). *The Arch Enemy of Economic Freedom*, self-published, p.6.

10 Herman E. Daly (1980). 'The Economic Thought of Frederick Soddy'. *History of Political Economy*, **12**(4), pp.473-4.

11 Ibid., p.474.

12 Frederick Soddy (1926). *Wealth, Virtual Wealth and Debt*, George Allen and Unwin Ltd., London, p.70.

13 Frederick Soddy (1934). *Money Versus Man*, Elkin Mathews & Marrot, London, p.28.

14 Ibid., p.24.

15 Frederick Soddy, *Wealth, Virtual Wealth and Debt*, op. cit., p.87.

16 Herman E. Daly, 'The Economic Thought of Frederick Soddy', op. cit., p.475.

17 This is explained fully in Richard Heinberg (2003), *The Party's Over*, New Society Publishers, Gabriola Island, Canada.

18 Albert A. Bartlett (2004). 'Thoughts on Long-Term Energy Supplies', *Physics Today*, July 2004, pp.53-5.

19 John Kenneth Galbraith [1958]. *The Affluent Society*. 40th Anniversary edition, 1998, Houghton Mifflin, New York, p.114.

20 John Maynard Keynes (1931). *Essays in Persuasion*, Macmillan, London.

21 Thorstein Veblen [1899]. *The Theory of the Leisure Class*, 1953-1959, Mentor Books, New York. First published by the Macmillan Company.

22 His use of *our grandchildren* in the title of the chapter, and *all of us* in the first line, implies to me that Keynes had only the descendants of the then-living inhabitants of the rich countries in mind.

23 Herman E. Daly and John B. Cobb (1990). *For the Common Good*, Merlin Press, London.

24 'Petroleum' is used here as shorthand for crude oil and natural gas. Coal reserves

are present in immense amounts, but an entire industrial infrastructure would have to be built to make it useful in transportation. At present the portability of petroleum products makes them the key to the world's economy.

25 One must distinguish between useful energy and total energy. According to the International Energy Agency (IEA), 6.9% of the world's total *primary* energy is provided by nuclear power. This is correct, but distorts the question of the nuclear share of *useful* energy. Nuclear fission produces heat energy, which can be used only for the generation of electricity – a transformation in which, from the Second Law of Thermodynamics, two-thirds of the heat energy is irrevocably wasted. This is a law of nature that innovation cannot 'break'. Correctly calculated, nuclear power supplies only 2.7% of the world's energy *use*. The large amount of heat generated can be safely used only for electricity generation, because of the safety requirement of absolute confinement of the highly radioactive coolant within the reactor building. Heat exchangers could in principle be used for space warming outside of the building, in order to utilize a part of the wasted energy, but the possibility of contamination through leakage would put large populations at risk.

26 S. Lorek and J. H. Spangenberg (2001). 'Reichtum und Umwelt'. In R. Rilling and K. Stadlinger (eds.) *Reichtum in Deutschland*, Westfälische Dampfboot, Münster, Germany.

27 Joachim H. Spangenberg (2001). 'The Environmental Kuznets Curve – A Methodological Artefact?'. *Population and Environment*, **23**(2) (November 2001), pp.175-91.

28 John Kenneth Galbraith [1958]. *The Affluent Society*. 40th Anniversary edition, 1998, Houghton Mifflin, New York. p.260.

Chapter 7

1 See Amartya Sen, *Development as Freedom* (1990), Random House, New York. It would not be appropriate here to go into a detailed examination of Sen's standpoint on development. In the last section of this chapter we examine in detail his views on labour and on markets in general, and explain why we hesitate to accept them carte blanche.

2 We do not wish to labour this point, but it might be helpful for the reader unfamiliar with the mode of thinking involved in Summers' analysis to point out that in mainstream economic thinking one calculates the cost of people dying, e.g. as a consequence of the dumping of poisons, by assigning a cost to each death equal to the (lifetime) earnings of the deceased. It is thus much less 'costly' when poor people die than when rich people die, and therefore better, economically, to poison the people in a poor country than in a rich country.

3 The basic change in World Bank policies and their effectiveness, effected by Wolfensohn from 1995 onwards, are discussed later.

4 John Perkins (2004). *Confessions of an Economic Hit Man*, Berrett-Koehler Publishers Inc., San Francisco.

5 M. Rosemeyer. (1997). 'Challenges to sustainable agriculture in Central America'. In P. B. Smith and A. Tenner (eds). *Dimensions of Sustainability*, Proceedings of

the Congress 'Challenges of Sustainable Development', Amsterdam, 22-25 August 1996. Nomos Verlagsgesellschaft, Baden-Baden.

6 Amartya Sen, *Development as Freedom*, op. cit.

7 Karl Polanyi (1994). *The Great Transformation*, Beacon Press, Boston.

8 Ibid., p. 7.

9 Polanyi, op. cit., p.77.

10 Sen, op. cit., p.6.

Chapter 8

1 J.C.L. Simonde de Sismondi [1819]. *New Principles of Political Economy*, Translated and annotated by Richard Hyse, 1990, Transaction Publishers, New Brunswick.

2 The faulty reasoning involved in the theoretical rule that lowering the interest rate will stimulate economic activity is nicely exposed in J. K. Galbraith's *Culture of Contentment* (1993), Penguin Books, Harmondsworth, pp.90-91.

3 De Sismondi, op. cit.

4 Ibid.

Chapter 9

1 In this book we take a billion to be one thousand million, and a trillion to be one million million.

2 Ideas for this section have been taken from Jerry Mander (ed.) (2007), *Manifesto on Global Economic Transitions*. The International Forum on Globalization, San Francisco.

3 A key source of information for this section was Caroline Lucas's and Colin Hines's 'Time to replace Globalization' (2002), a Green Localist Manifesto for World Trade, The Green/European Free Alliance in the European Parliament.

4 Adam Smith [1776]. *An Inquiry into the Nature and Causes of the Wealth of Nations*. Encyclopaedia Britannica edition, 1992, p.217. It is quite incredible that the concept for which Adam Smith is best known, 'the invisible hand', is simply a metaphor that appears in just one sentence in the entire original text of 1,000 pages.

5 John Gray (1998). *False Dawn: The Delusions of Global Capitalism*. Routledge, London.

6 David Korten (1995). *When Corporations Rule the World*. Kumarian Press, Sterling, Virginia, p.111.

7 Lucas and Hines, op. cit.

Chapter 10

1 David Sirota (2009). 'Business aims to relax bans on products made with child and slave labour'. World News Daily Information Clearing House. http://www. informationclearinghouse.info/article23951.htm.

2 Manfred Max-Neef (1991). *Human Scale Development*, The Apex Press, New York and London, p.16ff. This book has been declared by the University of Cambridge

as one of the 50 most important books on sustainability. (See University of Cambridge Programme for Sustainability Leadership, *The Top 50 Sustainability Books*, Greenleaf Publishing, 2009.)

3   Ibid.
4   Herman E. Daly and John B. Cobb (1989), *For the Common Good*, Beacon Press, Boston. Appendix.
5   Friends of the Earth. See: www.foe.co.uk/community/tools/isew/index.html.
6   Johan Rockström et al. (2009) 'A Safe Operating Space for Humanity'. *Nature*, **461** (24 September 2009), pp.472-5.
7   Wolfram Ziegler (1979). 'Ansatz zur Analyse der durch technisch-ziviliziertr Gesellschaften verursachten Belastung von Ökosystemen', *Lanwirtschaftliches Jahrbuch*, **56**, p.899. And Wolfram Ziegler (1992). 'Zur Tragfähigkeit ökologischer Systeme', *Wissenschaftliche Zeitschrift, Tächnisch Universität Dresden*, **41**, p.17.
8   H.-P. Dürr (1993). 'Living with an Energy Budget: The 1.5 Kilowatt Society', Max-Planck Institut für Physik, unpublished manuscript.

Chapter 11

1   In Chapter 10 we saw how the Genuine Progress Indicator for the US begins to decline in 1970.
2   Tom Eley, 'America, the land of inequality'. Global Research, 14 February 2010, Centre for Research on Globalization. http://www.globalresearch.ca/index. php?context=va&aid=17621.
3   Most of the following information has been taken from David de Graw, World News Daily Information Clearing House. http://www.informationclearinghouse. info/article24692.htm.
4   Ibid.
5   Ibid.
6   The Gini coefficient, based on the Lorentz curve, is a measure of income inequality. The higher the figure, the greater the inequality. For the purpose of comparison, the Scandinavian countries have a similar level of the Gini coefficient, at around 25.
7   David deGraw, AlterNet, 17 February 2010. http://www.alternet.org/module/ printversion/145705.
8   Ibid.

Chapter 12

1   Edward Fullbrook (2007). 'Economics and Neoliberalism'. In Gerry Hassan (ed.) *After Blair: Politics after the New Labour Decade*, Routledge, London.
2   Ibid.
3   The 1919 total solar eclipse was the opportunity for Sir Arthur Eddington to demonstrate the accuracy of General Relativity predictions.
4   Edward Fullbrook (2009). 'Toxic Textbooks'. In Jack Reardon (ed.) *The Handbook*

of Pluralist Economics Education, Routledge, London and New York.
5 Fullbrook, 'Economics and Neoliberalism', op. cit.
6 Geoffrey M. Hodgson (2008), 'How should the collapse of the world financial system affect economics?'. *Real-world Economics Review*, **48**, pp.273-8.
7 'Open letter from economic students to professors and others responsible for the teaching of this discipline'. http://www.paecon.net/PAEtexts/a-e-petition.htm. Ample information about the Post Autistic Economics movement and publications can be found at www.paecon.net.
8 'Petition for a Debate on the Teaching of Economics.' http://www.paecon.net/PAEtexts/Fr-t-petition.htm.

Chapter 13

1 'From the Village to a Global Order' was a programme launched by the Dag Hammarskjöld Foundation of Sweden in the early 1980s, under the sponsorship of which the Theories of Human Scale Development and of Fundamental Human Needs came into existence.
2 Paul Hawken (2007). *Blessed Unrest: how the largest movement in the World came into being and why no one saw it coming*. Viking Press, New York.
3 See Clive Hamilton (2003), *Growth Fetish*, Allen and Unwin, Sydney, Australia.
4 Paul Hawken, op. cit.
5 Paul Hawken, op. cit., Appendix.
6 Google shows about 300,000 pages for Human Scale Development.
7 Minga is an ancestral form of Indian cooperative organization, the purpose of which is to achieve conditions that benefit members of the community, or the community as a whole, through communal work.
8 ADC, in Spanish 'Asociación de Desarrollo Campesino'.
9 Sarah James and Torbjörn Lahti (2004). *The Natural Step for Communities: How Cities and Towns can Change to Sustainable Practices*, New Society Publishers, Gabriola Island, Canada.
10 Alliance for Sustainability: The Natural Step Framework's Four Conditions for Sustainability or 'System Conditions'. See http://homepages.mtn.org/iasa/tnssystemconditions.html.
11 Manfred Max-Neef (1991), *Human Scale Development*, The Apex Press, New York and London.
12 Avaaz is the name of the NGO that promoted the collection of signatures. It is concerned with many other initiatives of social justice.

Index